D0893291

WHAT TO DO WHEN THE RUSSIANS COME

WHAT TO DO WHEN THE RUSSIANS COME

RUSSIANS COME

A Survivor's Guide

Robert Conquest and **Jon Manchip White**

STEIN AND DAY/*Publishers*/New York

Copyright © 1984 by Robert Conquest and Jon Manchip White
All rights reserved, Stein and Day, Incorporated
Designed by Louis A. Ditizio
Printed in the United States of America
STEIN AND DAY/*Publishers*
Scarborough House
Briarcliff Manor, NY 1010

Library of Congress Cataloging in Publication Data

·Conquest, Robert.
    What to do when the Russians come.

    1. United States—Foreign relations—Soviet Union.
2. Soviet Union—Foreign relations—United States.
3. Communism—United States—1917-   . 4. United
States—National security.   5. Imaginary histories.
I. White, Jon Ewbank Manchip, 1924-   . II. Title.
E183.8.S65C66   1984   327.73047   84-40236
ISBN 0-8128-2985-9

CONTENTS

Foreword   9

1. The First Shock   15

2. Immediate Dangers: Prison and Labor Camp   33

3. Escape Abroad?   55

4. At Home   61

5. The Individual by Profession, Opinion, and Habit   77

6. The Quality of Life   145

7. Resistance   161

Afterword   175

A NOTE TO
THE READER

It is widely accepted that the United States now faces a real possibility of succumbing to the power of an alien regime unless the right policies are pursued.

It is not the purpose of this book to argue which policies are right. Its aim is quite different. It is, first, to show the American citizen clearly and factually what the results of this possible Soviet domination could be and how it would affect him or her personally; and second, to give some serious advice on how to survive.

How can you, the individual American citizen, expect your personal record to be treated by the new masters?

What kind of existence, under Soviet domination, can you look forward to?

Will there be any possibility of protest, resistance, and revolt; and what forms might they take?

This book offers you insights into what it will be like and advice as to survival behavior in the far-from-impossible event that this is what the future holds in store.

You should not take what we say as some horrible fantasy. Every word is based on the actual experience of hundreds of millions of ordinary people, in a dozen countries—people like yourself, most of whom had no more thought of the possibility of what actually happened to them than most Americans do today.

FOREWORD

Try to picture yourself as you might be in ten years time, perhaps less.

We are assuming that you are one of the lucky ones.

None of your family have been killed, except a distant cousin shot in the street early on, and your brother-in-law in the marines who was executed as a war criminal. None of the women have been raped.

Your job was one of the many that ceased to exist, and your savings have been extinguished by the "currency reform," but you had enough food and fuel to carry you through until you found your present low-paid post in one of the huge new rationing offices.

Your home was not wrecked or even damaged. And it was not impressive enough to be confiscated for the new elite or for Soviet officers. You escaped strangers being billeted on you by quickly settling into it a couple of families of friends who had lost theirs. You get on reasonably well, and although there is inevitable friction and the occasional flare-up, you are long since used to the overcrowding.

You had a tiring trip to work, changing twice between jam-packed buses; but it really is too far to bicycle. Once in the office things were fairly quiet, except that the ex-economics professor, who sweeps the floors and tidies up the washrooms, grumbled when they came around for the weekly compulsory contribution to the State Loan. How long can he last if he keeps doing that?

On your return journey you got your permit to visit your old parents in a neighboring state next month, after waiting only an hour. And when you drew the potato ration, you were pleased to find it was practically the right weight and of reasonable quality, capable of making a decent meal when you mix it with one of your bouillon cubes. What's more, while waiting in line for it, you met a friend who told you where some apples were available, and you hurried over there and managed to get a couple.

So here it is, only nine at night and you are already back home. You have not had time to look at the paper, but when you settle down to read it, there is little except news of Soviet industrial and artistic achievements and speeches by American Communists recently back from Moscow. You do notice an account of the trial of a dozen local officials for sabotage; but they are not from the Department of Agriculture, so this does not mean another famine. You start to remark on this, but you quickly break off. The children are around, and the younger ones might unthinkingly repeat what you say somewhere outside or at school.

Your ears catch the crunch of boots at the end of the street.

A Soviet platoon goes past. You automatically draw back still farther from the window. But it is only a routine patrol, not one of the special squads, so you relax as you see the helmets flickering in the red glow of the lone street lamp.

Yes, so far you have certainly been lucky. Next door, the old schoolteacher was arrested a few weeks ago for failing to abuse President Truman in a history lesson. Half a block away, the chairperson of the local Democratic party resisted arrest and was shot on the spot. (Her Republican opposite number, from another section of town, is in the uranium mines in Northwest Canada and rumored to be on the point of death.) The widow in the house across the way had a son in the FBI, who has vanished without trace. And the Chinese couple a little farther down have been deported. . . .

Suppertime. A delicious smell from the Primus stove—the potatoes are nearly boiling. Tomorrow is another day. Today, at least, has been uneventful . . . a good day.

This may not happen.
But, on the other hand, IT MAY . . .

How could such a state of affairs come about?

First, we will consider the ways in which, after the initial confrontation, the Soviets will establish their grip on the political organization of the United States and the ways in which this will affect the ordinary citizen.

Then, we shall deal with the most immediate dangers facing you if you are *not* one of the lucky ones: arrest and dispatch to a labor camp or exile, a fate that will not overtake everybody but one that will be common enough to be a very serious risk to almost all of you, affecting probably some 20 percent of the adult population. We seriously believe that the advice we give in this context, and on the possibility of escaping abroad, could save thousands of lives.

For those who have not been arrested, or not yet, we describe the problems of ordinary life, with advice on how to cope with them.

We go on, in chapter 5, to consider how particular people are likely to fare. For our readers are not merely citizens. They are farmers, industrial workers, doctors, students, clergymen; they are Republicans, Democrats, Socialists, "New Leftists"; they are Polish Americans, blacks, Chinese Americans, Jews: and they are all the other things Americans are.

We then analyze the quality of life: coping with the bureaucracy and with informers, crime and travel, conscription into the American People's Army for wars abroad, personal relations at home.

And we conclude with an examination of the prospects of resistance, in both the short and the long terms, concluding that it is even possible that some readers may survive to see the rebirth of freedom.

Let us repeat, everything we tell has been the experience of great populations. We are not even presenting a "worst case." We have not transferred to America the mass slaughters such as the Terror of 1937-1938 in the USSR, that have been inflicted in a number of Communist countries. Things may be worse than we have outlined. At any rate, they will hardly be better.

WHAT TO DO WHEN THE RUSSIANS COME

1

THE FIRST SHOCK

THERE ARE SEVERAL ways in which disaster might
strike America.

We cannot totally exclude an all-out nuclear war
that is so destructive that little is left of either side; or one in
which America is largely destroyed with far less Soviet loss,
resulting in the occupation by Moscow's troops of a ruined and
depopulated land—a scenario quite commonly found in Soviet
military literature.

Such near-total annihilation is hard to envisage, although it
would be irresponsible for anyone to ignore the possibilities. But
what seems more likely, given the Soviet achievement of effective
superiority, would be the crumbling of American resistance
either after a limited Soviet nuclear strike or simply under a
threat against which the United States would have become practically defenseless.

Military occupation, perhaps under a gradual and partially
camouflaged facade, would be inevitable. And, however done,
this would be accompanied by a slow but total Sovietization of
America.

Initially American surrender might not be given such a harsh name. America would be allowed to save a certain amount of face—whether it had to back down because of Soviet superiority of weapons or because it had lost an actual war—by disguising the unpleasantness of formal surrender under some such rubric as a "disarmament agreement." America would agree to the dispatch of Soviet "inspection teams" to monitor the "agreement." The teams would be military and would set up bases in key areas. Their consistent and rapid reinforcement, which the United States would be powerless to halt, would naturally lead, without undue loss of time, to full-scale Soviet control.

In the case of the three small Baltic countries of Estonia, Latvia, and Lithuania, which were once democratic republics, the Soviets began their expansion by demanding "defensive" bases. This was done in the guise of a "military defense pact." Ostensibly, this in no way intruded on the sovereignty or independence of the host countries. Within months, however, the Russians announced the discovery of "plots" against them, which required the total occupation of the states in question. A few weeks later "elections" were held, which not surprisingly resulted in a call for immediate annexation to the USSR. Each country was then placed under a special Soviet commissioner (one of whom was the veteran Mikhail Suslov, prominent in Moscow's councils until his recent death) and under a Soviet police chief. Between them they introduced the full rigor of the Communist system.

On the other hand, in Poland and most of the other countries of Eastern Europe, when the Russians took over during the heavy fighting in the last phase of World War II, they thought it best, instead of imposing their own system immediately, to set up transitional governments in which representatives of the old political parties—with all "anti-Soviet" elements removed—were permitted to serve until such time as it became expedient to suppress them. In each case the Russians made sure from the start that their Communist stooges controlled the police apparatus and all the machinery of repression. This is the likely pattern in the U.S.A.

The initial harshness of Soviet conduct in these circumstances depends on tactical considerations. At the moment, the Russians behave more roughly than they did ten or fifteen years ago but not as roughly as they did thirty years ago. They are still somewhat sensitive to presenting too repulsive an appearance to international audiences. But when the world is looking the other way (as to some degree in Afghanistan today), or during wartime, or in the turmoil of postwar circumstances, or when the globe has been sufficiently communized, complete ruthlessness has been and will be the order of the day.

If, in a few years' time, the occupation of the United States actually comes about, it will mean that any significant, freely informed world opinion will have ceased to carry weight. There will be almost nobody left to placate or gull or shock. Any inhibitions on tough behavior by the Soviet troops, police, or bureaucrats who occupy the United States will not be applicable. The Russians will behave as they like, according to their estimate of the comparative benefits of actual ruthlessness and apparent concession.

Is it possible to imagine a smooth acceptance of the fait accompli by a people so spirited and freedom-loving as the Americans? We would naturally expect that there will be much resistance, at least of a sporadic and disorganized nature. Individual citizens or the remnants of defeated army units will inspire desperate revolts, riots, strikes, and demonstrations against the incoming occupier. These will be savagely stamped out and will be followed by rampages of terror, looting, and rape by the Soviet troops.

This is not to say, in spite of the immediate suffering it will cause, that such hopeless resistance will not be of value to the country as a whole. It will serve to offset the demoralization of an

America that has been defeated or goes down without fighting. It will inspire those who will eventually begin to work and plan for the liberation of their country. Many of the early resisters will, moreover, in any case, be men who are bound to be rounded up and shot by the Russians in any case, and who will decide that it is better to die in a foxhole, fighting back, than in the cellars of the secret police after months of suffering.

Random shootings, homicidal incidents, executions—either of hostages or as a result of mistaken identity—and so on, will anyhow certainly be major problems for Americans. Even if the occupation has taken place in more or less peaceful circumstances and the Soviet army has been largely kept in hand, many acts of violence will inevitably occur.

Misunderstandings will arise because of the simple fact that most Americans do not speak Russian and most Russian soldiers do not speak English. There will be little means of communication except by means of fist and rifle butt. Another difficulty will arise because many Russians are heavy drinkers. Most American cities are well provided with liquor stores, and most American homes are well stocked with bottles. Drunken soldiers are not easy to cope with. They will be further elated by the enormous scope of their victory.

What are you, the ordinary citizen, to do?

Your best course is to lay in, as far in advance as you can, an ample supply of provisions (see chapter 4). In the first days of the occupation keep off the streets. Stay indoors. Keep away from the windows. Remain at the back of the house. Do not reply to any knock on the front door. If you hear your front door being broken in, try to smuggle your family out of an exit at the rear if you can do so without running into any patrols that may be prowling in the back.

You will, of course, be able to recognize members of the Soviet army by their uniform. Should you by some mischance encounter them in the open air or on the sidewalk, stand aside, or step off the curb, and keep your eyes down. Do not attempt any kind of heroics or dumb insolence. Russians are not famous for their sense of humor, and what sense of humor they possess is notoriously capricious. Take no liberties. These are mean people. In particular secret police troops—of whom there will be many— have done unspeakable things to their own countrymen, and there is no reason to suppose that they would not behave with a total lack of pity toward conquered Americans.

Judging by past performance, rape could be a major problem. Even if your city or area has been taken over without resistance, for the first three or four weeks you should expect massive and repeated incidents to occur. The women of your family should avoid letting themselves be seen outside the house or at the windows, if this is at all possible. Emergency hiding places should be provided for each of them in case of break-ins. As a precaution, we suggest that all the women in your family, from puberty to menopause, should begin to take the pill regularly when a Soviet occupation looks probable or even possible; in these circumstances, be prudent and lay in a sufficient stock. Women who are younger or older will not, of course, need such protection against unwanted pregnancy, although they will not thereby be exempted from the possibility of rape.

The usual procedure is for groups of five or six soldiers, or sometimes more, to enter a house, hold the males at gunpoint, and rape the females. In some parts of Central and Eastern Europe, the man of the house would attack the Russian intruders, and although he was killed, his action did result in a diminution of such assaults. Elsewhere in Europe the husbands and male relatives took the view that they would be needed later by their families and held themselves back. This led to less murder but more rape. Advice is difficult. The reaction will depend on the individual.

Note that a willingness to cooperate with the Soviet army does not carry with it immunity from rape. In Yugoslavia, local

Communists complained that some two hundred female secretaries of Communist organizations had been among the ravished.

You will have little defense against looting. If you go out, leave behind your watch or jewelry. It is even known for Soviet soldiers to demand jackets and shirts at gunpoint, so wear your oldest clothes. Remember that for these soldiers many things regarded as commonplace and as the everyday concomitants of American life will appear as new and marvelous. Looting of stores will probably be more general than the looting of homes; but you should be prepared for the latter. Hide anything of value, or anything you are going to need in the dark days ahead, if it is in any way possible to do so.

Incidentally, it is unwise to complain of looting or rape to the military authorities. It will do no good and may get you listed as a troublemaker. Moreover, in the ensuing period, the secret police will regard as particularly suspect anyone they know who has suffered at the hands of the Russians and who is hence likely to be an "unfriendly element."

It will not be the aim of the Russians to annihilate the American people but, rather, to reduce them to the status of loyal, or at least submissive, subjects of the puppet regime in Washington. The full rigor of the system will not be put into effect all at once; there will be no immediate Sovietization.

While ruthlessly suppressing open opposition and ensuring complete control of the police, the secret agencies, and all armed bodies, they will maintain a democratic facade, at least over a transitional period of several years. Under this cover, they will introduce the major changes in the social and economic order in a piecemeal manner with the grip gradually tightening.

After the first troubled months, there will thus be an interval when things seem to be cooling down, when there is some semblance of a return to "normality," when things appear to be at least tolerable and even "not so bad."

On the political side, the Soviets will promise that there will be no intention to interfere with, or even seriously to tamper with, the operation of American democracy.

In fact, it is probable that the first government following the American surrender will not even contain any open Communists. It will be a "coalition" of surviving Democrats, Republicans, and "Independents"—the latter being known as well disposed toward the USSR, but no more. In principle, the parties left in existence, purged of all anti-Soviet elements, will be designed to harness, as far as possible, the political energies of the various sections of the population. The new government will not even term itself "socialist," but will proclaim itself "democratic" in the old sense, as was done in most of Eastern Europe.

On what kind of people will the Russians rely at this stage of the occupation? Experience shows that in the moment of defeat, it is usual, however one may detest the enemy power, to place a good deal of blame for the disaster on one's own former government. Therefore, important politicians of quite honest character will be found who will have maintained, sincerely and over a long period, that the fatal confrontation with the USSR was America's fault. They will assert that America has brought the catastrophe upon itself, and they will in consequence claim that it is their moral duty to make the best of a bad job and ensure that some sort of American government continues. This was the position taken by many Frenchmen (whose basic patriotism was unquestioned) who chose to remain with Pétain and Vichy in 1940 instead of crossing the English Channel and joining de Gaulle and by many honest Eastern European democrats when Stalin's troops arrived. It is a genuine moral dilemma.

Such people will in effect assist the Russians in their immediate aim of securing a government temporarily acceptable to Moscow without, at the same time, being too repulsive to the people of the United States. In any case, stunned by calamity, Americans will scarcely know which way to turn.

We should also mention, not only the outright Quislings and Husáks, but the host of opportunists and eager collaborators who customarily come crawling out of the woodwork in such crises and often from the most unlooked-for directions. A few at least will turn out to have been long-term and devoted Soviet agents all along. This you will only learn years later when they write their memoirs and boast about the matter. Such self-revelations were made by several leading political figures in Eastern Europe, for example, Fierlinger in Czechoslovakia and Ronai in Hungary. Outwardly genuine Social-Democrats, although secretly Soviet agents, they rose high in the councils of their party with Russian support. They later went on record about the way in which they eventually got control of their parties and then dissolved them into the local Communist parties.

Blackmail, often of the crudest sort, will also be used in suborning the loyalties of politicians. Those politicians (and other public figures) who have something in their lives that they wish to conceal, and that has been discovered by the KGB, could be pliable instruments during the period of transition. Such men, who would not betray their country in wartime, not even to save their own reputations, may probably now be able to persuade themselves, under KGB prompting, that they can be "moderating influences." In Eastern Europe a number of "Agrarian," "Social-Democrat," and other figures of eminence were found to have been involved in financial or sexual scandals that the Soviets authorities kept quiet in exchange for their collaboration. The cases of Tonchev and Neikov in Bulgaria come to mind. In Western Europe, major leaders like Jouhaux, head of the French trade unions, and various other socialist and union figures in Britain and elsewhere, became puppets of Soviet blackmail and were compelled to steer their organizations in a direction indicated by the Communists. There are certainly some American figures who would be susceptible to such tactics.

In every sphere, people whom the Soviets consider useful as tools during the transitional era, even if they do not regard them as entirely trustworthy, will emerge. However, if you are considering a career as a collaborator, it is well to recollect that the Soviets are short on gratitude and that, as in Eastern Europe, within half a dozen years, the initial group of Soviet cat's-paws is bound to vanish, almost without exception, in decidedly sticky circumstances.

Meanwhile, the "new" American government, containing familiar and even respected faces, will give the appearance of constitutionality and the reassurance of continuity.

This appearance of constitutional continuity will involve a flurry of "by-elections" to fill the seats that have been vacated by men who have been executed, who have fled the country, or who have resigned in despair. The new candidates will be hand-picked by organizations that have already been purged of their "anti-Soviet" elements. Those likely to present an image of sturdy independence will be discouraged from presenting themselves as candidates by various effective means. The counting of the votes in such elections and by-elections will be done by committees selected with special care.

By this means, Congress and state and local bodies will be largely transformed into organs that offer no effective resistance to the consolidation of the new order. Even so, at first there will be men and women, even among the newly elected, who will begin to voice objections. They will be attacked in the media, harassed, and left for removal until the next "elections," by which time the whole political process will be under complete control and no awkward-minded senators or congressmen will remain to inconvenience the government. This will result in a wave of show trials in which the objectors will be charged with conspiracy to overthrow the government.

The death or deposition of the president and vice-president, assuming that they have not managed to flee the country, will be handled in the same way. Possibly it might not be necessary to execute or even depose them, at least at first; compromised by the responsibility of signing the instrument of surrender, they might prove to be acceptable figureheads during a brief transitional phase. They could of course be forced to resign or be impeached by a pliable Senate and replaced, in the manner provided for in the American Constitution, by a Speaker newly elected by a much-changed House of Representatives. But there might be time enough to get rid of them when the regular presidential election year arrives, when the outward appearance of traditional practice would be maintained.

The main thrust of the Russians will, of course, be behind the Communist Party of the United States. It will be confronted with a formidable task of organization. It will be given all the money, premises, and access to the media it requires and some control of security and other armed groups. Initially it will attract a swarm of recruits in the shape of careerists, but as an obvious stigma will attach to it in the minds of most Americans, it will quickly seek to expand itself by other means as well. After a short interim period, for example, it will attempt to merge with other organizations of the Left into a "united party" under effective Communist guidance. At this juncture, what you will probably see is a "Unity Congress," with a Socialist party splinter group pretending to be the entire party, a similar pseudorepresentation of the American Labor party based in New York, and a revived Farmer-Labor party, all funded and controlled by the Soviets and stiffened with Communist cadres. In addition any New Left groups that had previously been identified in any way with Leninism will be represented. Soon a merger between all these Leftist groupings will be arranged, under the name of the now fake

26

Farmer-Labor party or the equally fake Socialist party. In this way a respectable-looking basis for establishing a third major party under total Communist control would be provided, and the new party would enter into a "coalition" with the remains of the Democratic and Republican parties and gradually work toward dominating the whole state apparatus.

To begin with, the American Communist party will necessarily find itself somewhat shorthanded. We should note that, even on official figures, the Romanian Communists numbered only a thousand in a country of eighteen million and were nevertheless a mass party, in total control, with the usual set of puppet democratic parties only holding a few decorative posts, within a year of the arrival of the Soviet army.

It is of course not the case that there will be thousands and thousands of Americans who are suddenly converted to communism or show themselves to have been unsuspected sympathizers of it all the time. It will simply not be possible for the new rulers to operate entirely, or even to a very great extent, through the sort of people they would wish to have in charge. They will work, instead, through the careful establishment of Communists and others prepared, for whatever reason, to do their will in a comparatively limited number of key posts.

From these they will enroll, as far as possible, a broader section of the population, including those who have any favorable opinion whatever of the Soviet system or of its replicas in Vietnam and elsewhere and even of those who merely dislike the American system as it was before the Occupation, together with the unscrupulous and the ambitious.

It has been reckoned that, in any population, about 2-3 percent of the people in the country will be ready to carry out, for power and payment, the most revolting tasks that any regime whatever wishes to perform. The Communists could therefore certainly look forward to about a couple of million persons to staff their operations. This is a smallish number, but on the record of other countries, it will be found enough (with Soviet help) to provide a just adequate framework for administering and controlling factories, schools, offices, and municipalities.

Their control will be spread thin at first and gradually strengthen. If you are not favorably inclined to the new regime but have passively accepted it out of apathy or inability to see any alternative, you may find yourself a manager, school principal, or whatever. But you should note that your prospects of longer tenure are low.

Even when, by such methods, the Communist party has expanded to its maximum, membership will not be granted to all who wish to join. There comes a point at which the party is big enough to control the country and holds all the posts with even the slightest influence down to township level; then recruitment will ease off, and purging and discipline of the new membership will become intense (see chapter 5).

Under the party, as its youth subsidiaries, will be two much bigger organizations (already in existence), the Young Communist League and the Pioneers.

The Young Communist League will be extended to enroll millions of young people in their teens and early twenties, and membership will be a virtual requisite for a large number of jobs above the most menial. Its branches will be under the control of party members, and all Young Communists will be required to obey party orders, to attend indoctrination sessions, and to operate as an arm of the party in their schools, streets, and homes.

The Pioneers are a sort of ghastly parody of the Scouts and Guides and were consciously so right from the start. They will be virtually compulsory for all preteenage schoolchildren. The Pioneers will be subjected to a simple style of propaganda, be given many attractions, go to indoctrination-infested summer camps, and have various solemn ceremonies in which, for example, they dip their richly embroidered flags in the memory of Lenin and take oaths of loyalty to the organization and its aims.

28

The whole apparatus of state legislatures, city councils, and so forth, will continue. But you will get used to the idea that the real power in your neighborhood is not in the hands of these officials but in those of the local party secretaries. Legislatures, including Congress in Washington itself, will meet less and less frequently until it is a matter of no more than five or ten days a year that they will be in session to unanimously pass bills laid before them by the Communist authorities.

As one of the principal agencies of restraint, the new government will be able to rely, of course, on a totally reorganized FBI—for it is possible that the old name will be kept, again for purposes of continuity, although behind the facade, the whole organization will have been virtually dissolved (and all operatives who have been concerned with preventing subversion or countering Soviet espionage are liable to be shot). If those present in the top echelons have the time and the opportunity, it is to be hoped that they have already made arrangements to destroy all sensitive files, in order that agents now working under cover may have some chance of survival. Similarly, the names and dossiers of left-wing but anti-Soviet activists, who might help to provide a nucleus of anti-Soviet resistance, should not be allowed to fall into the hands of the Russians, who are likely to be unprecedentedly thorough in their elimination of such persons.

In any case, the new secret police, whether called the FBI or not, will be staffed entirely by totally reliable Soviet agents and will be supervised by Russian "advisers" who will be vested with full authority. It will be enormously expanded and will be provided with its own paramilitary formations.

As for the all-important question of controlling the organs of public information, the suppression of a selected number of newspapers, magazines, television and radio stations will be "demanded" because they have been the organs of "warmongers," and their premises and facilities will be delivered up to the Communist party. Other newspapers, magazines, television and radio stations not placed immediately under Communist control will continue to appear for some time, provided they have purged their staffs adequately and can secure the raw materials and other necessities they require in a time of dire scarcity. But they will all, of course, be strictly censored to make sure that nothing anti-Soviet or antigovernment appears.

Within a matter of months, all modes of mass communication will retail no news or information except that which conforms totally to the pro-Soviet line. For years to come, you will read or hear nothing but dreary praise (full of falsified statistics) for the Soviet Union and for the progress made by the new United States. Entire editions and newscasts will be given over to the texts of speeches by Soviet dignitaries and their American followers. Authentic news will be largely absent, and what there is will be highly dubious. This boring mishmash will occasionally be enlivened by accounts of the trials of "war criminals"— American political and military figures accused of waging, or merely planning, war against the USSR. You should not be surprised to find personages for whom you entertain the greatest admiration confessing to barbarities of which you rightly believe them to be incapable. You must remember that they will have been in secret police hands for a minimum of several months.

In the absence of reliable printed or broadcast news, if you wish to remain well informed, you will have to rely on rumor and on foreign broadcasts. Needless to say, not all of the rumors will be true, and many will have been deliberately planted by the authorities.

You will have to develop a feeling for the plausibility or implausibility of anything you hear. Does it seem probable? Does it fit in with other information? Often you will have to suspend judgment until some later piece of information confirms or refutes what you have heard.

You should also develop the knack, common in all Communist countries, of expertly reading between the lines of the official press. Attacks on officials of the Department of Agriculture, for example, taking them to task for mismanagement, probably presages a food shortage or even a famine. Particularly sharp concentration on the evils of China or some other foreign country may well imply that war is contemplated. And so on. You will become adept at interpreting the nuances of the official clichés.

Just as you must take great precautions when listening to foreign broadcasts (if you possess a set powerful enough to pick them up), so you must be very cautious, when it comes to unofficial information or rumor, of whom you listen to and to whom you pass it on. Merely to receive "hostile" information without reporting the "rumormonger" to the police is a criminal offense. To transmit it is worse. However, except in the case of news particularly offensive to the Soviet authorities, you should not encounter too much trouble if you are reasonably circumspect (unless the authorities are looking for some pretext to arrest you anyway). After all, almost everyone, including the local Communists and even the police, will have no alternative except to rely on, and subsequently to spread, that same material. They will live in the same fog that you do.

2

IMMEDIATE DANGERS: PRISON AND LABOR CAMP

SOME OF THE dust, atomic or otherwise, of the conflict and its immediate aftermath has now settled, and the new administration has taken over your town.

The first thing you should bear in mind is that you and your family will face a constant threat of arrest and disappearance either into the labor camps or into the execution cellars.

As we shall see, large numbers of Americans will be doomed to arrest, in any event. For the rest of the populace, it will be largely a matter of luck—although you can temper your fate, at least to some degree, by trying to understand the predicament in which you have landed and attempting to make a swift adjustment to it.

We can by no means guarantee that readers of this book will be among the survivors, but at least, we offer some tips that might mean that their chances will be considerably improved.

Arrest

The majority of American citizens are patriotic, naturally

outspoken, and innately opposed to the idea of dictatorship. Many frank remarks will be made in the early months of the occupation that will very soon be bitterly regretted.

The Soviet authorities will not, of course, be able to arrest everybody, but since it will be necessary to repress and deter hostile thought and action, the number of arrests will obviously run into millions.

In a "difficult" country like America, where the tradition of liberty has been strong, the probability is that, apart from executions, about 25 percent of the adult population will ultimately be sent to forced-labor camps or exiled under compulsory settlement in distant desert and arctic regions or in the USSR. If past performance is anything to go by, around 5 percent of the prisoners in the labor camps would be women, although in a country like the United States, where women are so influential and play such a prominent role in the national life, the figure may be much higher.

In these circumstances, you will have given thought to the future of your children.

Sometimes, particularly in the early days, it will be usual for children to go to relatives should both their parents be arrested. If you have been unable to make such an arrangement in advance or no such relatives are available, the probability is that they will survive as members of gangs of urchins living on their wits, subject to arrest and incarceration in adult jails as soon as they are in their teens.

Later, State orphan homes, often barely distinguishable from reformatories, will be set up for such children. There they will be indoctrinated in Communist beliefs and, later, if suitable, sent to serve in the police and other units.

You should seriously consider how you can best equip your children for both spiritual and physical survival should they become lost or orphans. First, like yourselves, the rule is to be fit, not fat. When things start to look menacing, your relations with them must be particularly warm and trusting for they will only have you to turn to in a world that is becoming filled with suspicion and hatred and where nobody can be expected to talk freely and honestly. You will have to balance the necessity of never saying anything that they might innocently blurt out in front of unreliable acquaintances or known agents of the regime, against the need to ensure that their basic attitudes towards their country, their religion, and their parents remain as firm as is possible. It will be difficult for you and equally difficult for your children. But remember that experience shows that, on the whole, children remain loyal to their parents' teaching and example long years after the parents themselves have vanished. They will adapt very quickly to the new conditions and learn how to keep their real attitudes concealed while conforming outwardly to the official cult. With younger children, on the other hand, it may be that they will forget their parents completely. Even so, when they grow and find out for themselves what the real nature of the regime is, any seed you may have planted of a positive kind may still be there, ready for events to help it flower. In Soviet-occupied countries, it has been the young who have formed the core of mass resistance whenever that has become feasible.

You can only do your best, and hope and pray for their future. If you are lucky, and survive, it may even be possible for you to trace your lost ones and, against all the odds, be united with them in fifteen or twenty years' time.

The first wave of arrests and deportations will be inflicted not on the ordinary citizen but on outstanding and major figures, who will be seized as "war criminals." They will include political leaders and military men with a record of urging or heading resistance to communism in the international sphere.

The next wave, more gradual and broader, will extend to community leaders of every sort, particularly those who may have had any kind of international connections through travel, correspondence, or in the course of business. We might quote the official Soviet list of people subject to what was officially termed "repression" in the Baltic states when they were Sovietized. Among the various categories were the following:

- All former officials of the State, the army, and the judiciary
- All former registered members of the non-Communist political parties
- All active members of student organizations
- Members of the National Guard
- Refugees (from the USSR)
- Representatives of foreign firms
- Employees and former employees of foreign legations, firms, and companies
- Clergy
- People in contact with foreign countries, including philatelists and Esperantists
- Aristocrats, landowners, merchants, bankers, businesspeople, owners of hotels and restaurants, and shopkeepers
- Former Red Cross officials.

Since the danger of arrest is therefore substantial, whether you are "innocent" or not, we would advise you to be prepared for it at all times.

If arrested, you will probably be allowed to take a small package or a small suitcase with you, although all portable goods will eventually, with the connivance of the transport guards or camp guards, be stolen from you. (If you are merely being deported into exile and forced to reside in distant parts, you may even be permitted to take up to fifty pounds of baggage, although this too will be liable to theft.) However, it is always sensible to have bags packed and ready, so that you are not taken by surprise. At least compile a list, in order not to omit some essential item in the confusion of arrest. And, summer or winter, always keep a couple of pairs of good solid shoes and several pairs of socks handy. A quick-witted wife has often saved her husband's or son's life in Communist countries by keeping shoes, socks, gloves, scarf, and a warm overcoat handy. Remember that, if you can manage to hang on to them, minor articles of clothing can also be exchanged later for a loaf of bread in case of extreme need in prison or camp or on the journey there.

What pattern can you expect your arrest to follow?

We quote a typical official instruction from the Baltic states, although this applies to the arrest and deportation of whole families:

> Operations shall begin at daybreak. Upon entering the home of the person to be deported, the senior member of the operative group shall assemble the entire family of the deportee into one room. It is also essential, in view of the fact that large numbers of deportees must be arrested and distributed in special camps or sent to distant regions, that the operation of removing both the head of the household and the other members of his family shall be carried out simultaneously, without notifying them of the separation confronting them.

If you refuse to answer the door or to open it, it will be broken down. The operatives may or may not be provided with "search" and "arrest" warrants, but if they are, these are likely to be of a perfunctory and reusable variety. If the intention is to subject the arrestee to a propaganda show trial, as is occasionally the case, "evidence" will be planted on him or on the premises (like the one thousand German marks and one hundred American dollars planted in a cupboard of Ginzburg's apartment when he was arrested in January 1977).

What will happen to you when you have been taken to prison in a car, van, or truck?

First, you will be taken, after being briefly booked, straight to a prison cell. This could be in an improvised building, since the local prisons may be full to overflowing. You must not expect to enjoy the amenities of everyday American prison existence, where only a handful of men are placed in a single cell.

In the first great waves of mass terror, the crowding in prisons will be terrific. In the Soviet Union, it is common to read of from 70 to 110 people in cells designed barely to hold 25. When the overflow gets too great, it is likely, as in Soviet provincial towns, that vast pits will be dug and roofed over and prisoners simply herded in.

Washing will be a problem. For example, 110 women in one cell were allowed forty minutes with five toilets and ten water taps. The diet and general conditions will be unhealthy; prisoners will show a peculiar grayish blue tinge from confinement without light and air. Dysentery, scurvy, scabies, pneumonia, and heart attacks will be common and gingivitis universal.

Traditionally, on first arriving, you will find yourself occupying the spot next to the sinkhole or slop pail, but in the course of time, as the previous prisoners are taken out, you can expect to move up to a superior location.

At this stage of your incarceration, your wife, if she is able to find out where you are, will be allowed to come to the prison (though not to visit you there) in order to pay over small sums to the prison authorities with which, if they reach you, you may be able to buy such items as cigarettes and sugar. She may also be allowed to hand in packages of food and clothing.

You must do your best to adjust to the chaotic conditions and to accustom yourself to the fact that your prospects of release are almost nonexistent. You will have been considered guilty from the very fact of your arrest. Resign yourself to being held for an average length of time of from one to three months in your present situation.

Interrogation

You will be required to make a confession to one or more crimes against the State.

The Soviet secret police use three main methods to obtain confessions. If you are, as is unlikely, important enough to be marked down for a show trial, the long-term system of breaking your personality, which has become known as "brainwashing," will be applied. This involves a minimum of about three months with every possible physical and psychological pressure, especially inadequate food, inadequate sleep, inadequate warmth, and constant interrogation. Evzen Loebl, one of the Czech prisoners who confessed in the notorious Slansky trial and had the luck not to be hanged, describes having to be on his feet eighteen hours a day, of which sixteen were under interrogation, and during the six-hour sleep period having to get up and report every ten minutes when the warden banged on the door. After two or three weeks, he ached all over, and even washing became a torture. Finally, he confessed and was allowed food and rest, but by this time, as he put it, "I was quite a normal person—only I was no longer a person."

The chances are, however, that you will be made to confess by more time-saving methods. These are (often in combination) beating and the "conveyor" (that is, continuous interrogation without sleep for periods up to five or six days).

These methods are not infallible, and there have always been a few prisoners whom they did not break (and many more who, although confessing under these pressures, repudiated the confession when they recovered.)

41

As for the effects of beating and torture, we recommend the accounts by American prisoners of war in Hanoi, who were regularly tortured to betray the means of communication set up between them. There is a limit to almost anyone and no need to be ashamed if you give in.

Advice is difficult. Nevertheless, your chances of saving your life will be improved if you firmly decide not to confess to a capital offense. Interrogation machinery will be severely stretched, and it may be that your interrogator, to save time, will accept a confession of some lesser crime like "anti-Communist propaganda," which will only earn you five to eight years in a labor camp if you hold out long enough. Never, under any circumstance, believe promises that if you confess to capital crimes, you will be reprieved.

Your other problem—this time one of conscience—will be that you will be asked to name "accomplices." Try to use names of people you know are dead or have escaped the country or otherwise disappeared. In addition, you may be able to involve Communists or other Quislings.

You will eventually be sentenced, though not necessarily in your own presence—the judgment may merely be a smudged form handed you by a warden. Then, assuming you have avoided execution, you will be packed off to a labor camp.

Labor Camps

The trip, in tightly sealed cattle trucks, may last some weeks; and since the labor camp system will at first be more or less unorganized, you are likely to find that you and your companions are simply dumped, in the heat of the summer or the cold of winter, in a wooded area, where you will forthwith be set to work to build your own camp. Meanwhile you will live in a pit dug in the ground and covered with a canvas sheet.

One of the most likely sites for a great concentration of labor camps is in the uranium-bearing area of the Canadian Northwest Territories. There, as in similar projects in the USSR, climatic and other conditions are so hostile that it is hard to attract free labor except by the payment of astronomical wages. In America, too, the Soviet authorities will be able to draw upon an inexhaustible supply of forced laborers. Forced labor will also be employed in other areas of difficult exploitation or where massive unskilled labor is advantageous (for example, in working the oil-bearing shale beds of the American West). We can also expect forced-labor battalions to be put to work in Greenland and, in particular, in exploiting the coal and other deposits of Antarctica, where Soviet rule is likely to have been established by default. If, as is often stated, these deposits prove to be immensely rich, we may expect hundreds of thousands of American prisoners to be sent to work them, with the added advantage that the prisoners' whereabouts will be quite unknown at home. Conditions there may be expected to be extremely adverse, the work exhausting, and the prospects of survival negligible. Northern Canada, where the death rate will be high by all normal standards, would be a Utopia in comparison.

Uranium mining, however unpleasant, is at least rational. Many of you will find yourselves wasting your lives on projects whose only justification is the grandiose self-importance of political leaders or planners. For here, as everywhere else in the Soviet-type "planned economy," there will be enormous and idiotic waste. In the Soviet Union, a quite unnecessary and uneconomic Arctic railway to the town of Igarka was labored at for four years in temperatures down to −55° Centigrade in winter, by scores of thousands of prisoners in more than eighty labor camps, at intervals of 15 kilometers along the 1300-kilometer stretch. In the end, only 850 kilometers of rail and of telegraph poles had been built, and then the line and signals, the locomotives, and everything else were abandoned to rust in the snow. In

Romania, hundreds of thousands of prisoners' lives were lost in the Dobruja marshes, building a grandiose "Danube-Black Sea Canal" that was similarly abandoned. And there are many lesser tales of wasteful and useless projects dreamed up by stupid careerists trying to make a name. It will be little consolation to you to know that, when such a project fails, its originator may not be able to escape the search for scapegoats and end up in a camp himself or even be shot for "sabotage."

Wherever you are sent, you will find yourself working up to sixteen hours a day, from the 5 A.M. reveille, ill clad and undernourished. Even today, in the peacetime USSR, labor-camp ration scales are well below those issued by the Japanese in the notorious prisoners-of-war camps on the River Kwai (which averaged 3,400 calories a day against the Soviet 2,400).

How are you to prepare yourself for this?

If you at present perform a desk job or follow some other sedentary occupation, it is vital that you make yourself fit and ready for hard manual labor. In all the Communist countries, it has always been found that professors, lawyers, administrators, and officials are among the first people to succumb in the labor camps, where they are suddenly faced with intense physical exertion on inadequate rations.

You might also begin to practice a few skills that might possibly save you, once you are in the camps, from the most burdensome and debilitating work. For example, you might be able to stay alive if you were to take a first-aid course since you could then become a camp medical orderly or nurse. Doctors, subject to the limitations that will be noted later, would enjoy an automatic advantage. A few other professions might prove similarly beneficial. If you are an artist, for instance, the staff of the forced-labor camp will possibly employ you for such tasks as painting the numbers on prisoners' jackets, and so on, while senior camp officials have often been known to award painters a higher ration in return for paintings to decorate their quarters.

There is one problem that we ought to mention that will concern the relatives of the people who have been arrested. It is this. They are likely to find themselves approached by the secret police with the proposition that they will gain better treatment for the arrested member or members of their family, or perhaps even save them from execution, if they will become police informers and report on the work and private life of their friends.

When this happens, it will present you with a nasty moral dilemma. All the same, it might help you to bear in mind that such promises to ease the lot of arrested relatives have never, in Communist countries, been honored. In any case, the local branch of the secret police will have no control over what goes on in a labor camp hundreds, or even thousands of miles away. Once in the camps, your relatives are in a different world, almost on another planet, and beyond your ken.

Allied to this will be a further ordeal, affecting all rather than merely the closest relatives of the arrested person. Once your husband (for example) has been found guilty and sentenced as an enemy of the people, you, as his wife, together with your children, will be required to repudiate and denounce him. At school, your children will be required to go up and stand beside the teacher's desk and make a public condemnation and repudiation of their father. This is standard practice everywhere in Communist countries.

In the early phases, when the grip of the occupiers is being tightened to the limit, or after rebellions or other crises, the maximum Soviet terrorist methods will be used. At other times, there may be comparative relaxation. Perhaps we should give you some examples from the *present* situation in the Soviet

Union, when the country is at peace and wishes to avoid making a bad impression in the Western world.

In June 1977, a group of former Soviet prisoners who had managed by one means or another to reach safety in the West gave evidence at a hearing that was conducted at the Institute of Physics at Belgrave Square in London. The hearing was trying to accumulate evidence that might eventually assist in the case of Professor Yuri Orlov, a Soviet physicist who had been arrested in February 1977 on unspecified charges and was being held without trial. Extracts from the hearing were later published in the journal *Index* (November-December 1977).

Among those who testified were former inmates of (1) a Soviet prison, and (2) a Soviet labor camp.

Let us allow Vladimir Bukovsky, who underwent his most recent spell of incarceration in the Vladimir prison, to speak first.

I am 34 years old. I have been arrested four times because I expressed opinions which were not acceptable to the Soviet authorities. In all I have spent more than eleven years in prison, camps and psychiatric hospitals.

I spent a long time in Vladimir prison. The normal cells there have iron screens on the windows so that no ray of light can penetrate. The walls of the cells are made of rough concrete so they cannot be written on. They are damp. There is a heating system, but part of the punishment is to keep it deliberately low even in wintertime. The guards shove food through a trap door.

Sometimes the cells have no lavatories at all, only a bucket. Sometimes there is just a hole in the floor without any separation from the sewage system: all the stench from the sewage system thus comes back inside the cells, which have no proper ventilation system.

In punishment cells the conditions are worse. You are kept in solitary confinement in a room which is about 2½ sq.m. The only light is from a small bulb in a deep niche in the ceiling.

At night you sleep on wooden boards raised a few inches off the ground without any mattress or blankets or pillow. You are not allowed to have any warm clothing. Often there is no heating at all in winter. It is so cold that you cannot sleep, you have to keep warm by jumping up and running around your cell to keep warm.

At 6:00 o'clock in the morning your wooden bed is removed and there is nothing for you to do for the rest of the day, no newspaper to read, no books, no pen or pencil or paper—nothing.

According to the regulations a prisoner can only be put in solitary confinement for fifteen days, but quite often when one fifteen-day period ends prisoners are put back in for another fifteen days. I was lucky, because although I was in solitary confinement several times, I only had fifteen days at a time. Others were not so fortunate. It is quite customary for people to spend forty-five days in solitary.

In solitary confinement prisoners get a specially reduced diet. This is part of the punishment which I received in Vladimir prison in 1976 after Mr. Brezhnev had signed the Helsinki Declaration. On alternate days I had nothing to eat or drink except a small piece of coarse black bread and some hot water. On the other days I had two meals—in the middle of the day—some watery soup with a few cabbage leaves, some grains of barley, sometimes two or three potatoes. Most of the potatoes were black and bad. In the evening I had gruel made from oatmeal or some other cereal, a piece of bread and several little fish called *kilka*, which were rotten. However hungry I was, I could not eat them. That was all.

The shortage of food, the poor quality of the food you are given, and the appalling living conditions mean that almost everyone who has endured imprisonment suffers from stomach ulcers, enteritis or diseases of the liver, kidneys, heart, and blood vessels.

When I was first arrested I was very healthy, but after I had been in prison I too began to suffer from stomach ulcers and cholecystitis. This did not make any difference to the way I was treated. I was still put in the punishment cell on a reduced diet.

I was in the same cell with Yakov Suslensky, who suffers from a heart condition. He had a severe heart attack in an isolation cell, but was not taken out of isolation. He was moved, but only to another isolation cell. After he came out of isolation he had a stroke. This was in March 1976.

I was also in Vladimir prison with Alexander Sergienko who had tuberculosis. Notwithstanding this he was put in solitary confinement on a reduced diet.

I was also in prison with Mikhail Dyak, who suffers from Hodgkin's disease. He was released early, but not until three years after confirmation of his diagnosis. I knew many other people who were not released even though they had cancer and other serious illnesses.

In prison you are allowed to send out one letter a month, but the authorities can deprive you of that. If prisoners try to describe their state of health or the lack of medical help in prison, their letters are confiscated.

In prison hospitals essential medicines are often not available. I remember in 1973 a man named Kurkis who had an ulcer which perforated. There was no blood available to give him a transfusion. He lay bleeding for 24 hours and then he died.

Next, we might take the experiences of Andrei Amalrik, who described what life is like in a labor camp.

The strict regime camp of Kolyma is 300 kilometres north of Magadan, where the winter lasts eight months and is very harsh: the temperature varies between 20 and 60 degrees Centigrade below zero.

The camp is surrounded by several rows of wire. Inside the wire are two wooden fences, and dogs patrol the space between them. The camp is divided into a living compound and a work compound. In the living compound are four barrack huts accommodating eight hundred prisoners.

All the prisoners have to wear uniforms made of thin grey cloth and very thin boots. Everyone has their name and number sewn on their clothes. You march everywhere in columns.

Prisoners are fed three times a day. Breakfast is a sort of thin porridge, dinner is soup. Those who have fulfilled their work norm get extra porridge. The soup is very poor and has very few vitamins. That is why most of the prisoners are ill.

Prisoners work in the machine and furniture factories where the dust fills your lungs, or outside cutting wood and in the construction brigades.

It is difficult enough to work outside when the temperature is less than minus 20 degrees Centigrade; at minus 50 or 60 degrees the conditions are almost unimaginable. When it is as cold as that there is a sort of dry fog, which means that if you extend your arm, you cannot see your hand. Yet every day you have to go out and work (with the exception of only one day when I was in camp). It is so cold that many prisoners suffer inflammation of the ear, which can lead to loss of hearing. You are allowed to wear extra clothing or a fur cap. I made a band to go over my ears out of some socks, but the guards believed that I must be wearing this so I could listen to the BBC, which of course was nonsense.

I was put in a punishment cell on two occasions. Once in prison and once in camp. I was in a cell by myself. The cell was 1.5 m. wide and 2.5 m. long. The bed in the cell was made of wood. It was attached by hinges to the wall. In the daytime it was raised up and locked against the wall. The only thing to sit on was the concrete block on which the bed rested.

When I was put in the punishment cell my usual clothes were taken away and I was made to wear specially thin clothes. There were no books. You were allowed to smoke. I was given warm food only every other day and then it was of very poor quality. On the other days I just had bread and water.

In the punishment cell the heating was very low and there was a

49

window, but it had no glass in it, so that the intense cold came right into the cell. It was impossible to sleep. You had to keep moving about all night in order to keep warm.

I was lucky. I only spent five days in the punishment cells. The usual period was fifteen days. Frequently people spent fifteen days in the punishment cells, were let out for one day and then put back for a further fifteen days. Repeated solitary confinement means the slow destruction of the human body. Your personality is slowly destroyed.

Medicines are very poor and very few. In the camp where I was, there was one doctor who was not well qualified, one male nurse and one female nurse, whose objective was to see that people went to work.

And remember that these cases occurred in a comparatively relaxed period, in peacetime. You may expect worse, expecially, in the first flush of mass terror. Indeed, we are almost ashamed to have described conditions that appear idyllic compared with those likely to prevail, as they always have done in similar circumstances, when America is subjected to full-scale terror.

Apart from prison and labor camps, there is a third, although more unlikely, possiblity. After ten or fifteen years, assuming things are calmer, the authorities may begin to want some genuine-sounding excuse for the arrest and maltreatment of suspects; in this case a few of you may find yourselves subjected to the latest Soviet refinement: the pseudopsychiatric hospital. In these, as evidence from former inmates and former staff alike make clear, people whose only madness is to dislike communism are declared schizophrenic and injected with chemicals such as haloperidol and sulphazine, without the supplementary drugs necessary to prevent the extremely painful side effects—all under the supervision of the secret police. This would be a very nasty experience but not usually a fatal one, although some who have been released say they have never properly recovered. However, the numbers subjected to this particular horror would be comparatively few.

What lessons might you, as a prospective Soviet convict, derive from what we have told you?

Obviously there is no guaranteed method of survival in a Communist camp, prison or "mental hospital." The odds are against you. Nor will you be helped by the fact that the widespread dislocation that is bound to attend the first few years of Soviet rule in the United States will inevitably result in food and other shortages in the camps and prisons. They will be desperately overcrowded.

How are you to give yourself the best possible chance?

To begin with, try to be prepared psychologically. From the moment that your Government signs the instrument of surrender, always assume that the worst will happen to you. That way, you will not be betrayed by optimism and will not go into a state of shock or apathy at the moment that you are arrested.

Next, when you are in prison or in the camp, it is vital not to miss any opportunity to eat. This will not be easy since the experience of being thrown into jail will be enough to take away your appetite, and you have seen that even Vladimir Bukovsky could not wolf down, ravenous as he was, those stinking *kilka*. But you must try to force yourself to eat whatever swill is handed to you, especially in those first few days or weeks, otherwise you are quickly going to lose the physical reserves without which you cannot possibly survive. Be ready to eat anything. In the end, you will discover that you will have no choice, anyway, so the earlier you get used to the idea and swallow down your nauseating slop, the better.

Again, when it comes to the backbreaking labor that you will be assigned, remember that surviving will once again depend on your physical reserves. Some camps will probably be death camps, designed to use up a man's strength in anywhere between six weeks and six months, and in that case, there will be very little you can do since you will be fed a restricted diet. Even there, however, you will probably want to try to save your energy at all costs. Do everything as slowly as you can possibly get away with—such is the advice of all the survivors of the Soviet camps. Practice extreme slow motion. When you are lumbering, you might adopt the traditional trick of managing to get the same log counted by the guard several times by the expedient of sawing off the check number after each inspection. In most camps it has usually been possible, at least for a time, for separate labor gangs to cooperate in methods to claim a higher productivity than is really achieved. Remember that with every swing of your ax you are chopping an hour off your own life.

In one respect, strangely enough, you may after all be luckier than prisoners in the Soviet Union itself. You may find that in your camp the criminal element, with which every camp will be deliberately seeded, will not have the violence and customary solidarity of the Russian *urka* or criminal class. So you may discover that, although the American criminals in your camp have been encouraged by the prison authorities to take control and knock you about from the earliest moment of your arrival, it seems at least feasible that a determined and immediate lead by a group of your most vigorous "politicals" may result in the collapse of this form of exploitation. Even within the USSR itself, such a development has occasionally been noted as when a group of tough ex-soldiers, or really stubborn Ukrainian nationalists, have decided to stand up and assert themselves.

Although such a course presents certain dangers, and each situation must be judged on its merits, and there will be ugly scuffles and murders, we would urge you to assume instant readiness for such an opportunity. Otherwise, the acceptance of criminal supremacy will mean robbery gang rape, and a general reign of terror; besides leaving the cooking, control, and distribution of food in the hands of crooks, who will grab the biggest share of your already inadequate rations. Such a lack of boldness at the outset will therefore result in your death from dystrophy a few weeks later.

We seriously urge you, while you still can, to go to your local library and check out whatever books it contains on life in the camps. The works of Solzhenitsyn, and such books as Evgenia Ginzburg's *Into the Whirlwind* and General Gorbatov's *Years Off My Life* could prove useful guides. Do not read them as literature, or as accounts of alien experiences, but in the light of practical blueprints of a not-improbable future.

3

ESCAPE ABROAD?

T HE OPTION TO escape will not be open to many, but if you are in any of the categories doomed to virtually certain death, you are advised to take it if the opportunity should arise.

It is possible, even probable, that some non-Communist countries will remain unoccupied.

The conquest of the United States will of course make the USSR the world's dominant power, and there will no longer be much question of its ability to take over the world. But there will be good arguments against seeking to achieve this immediately. The Soviets will have strained their military resources to the limit and will be spread thin holding down their vast new empire. There will no longer be any great hurry in dealing with the remnants of "capitalism." While it is probable that Africa and the Middle East will now be under Soviet control and that the Russians will be involved in a general move forward in South America, they will have several motives for leaving other countries under threat and pressure, without yet moving to take them over.

They may even leave Western Europe, or part of it, uninvaded, as now impotent to harm and politically bypassed to wither on the vine. There would be good economic reasons for this in that the powerful capitalist productivity of these countries will be needed to make up for the old inefficiencies and the new dislocations of the Soviet-occupied world, providing products beyond the skill of the Soviets—just as, today, Finland has been left un-Sovietized, as a valuable trading partner.

It is also wholly possible that China will not yet have been reduced, since that will in any case involve a further enormous military effort, to say nothing of the probability of the Soviet army getting bogged down in a partisan war that would make America's recent problems in Vietnam small in comparison.

However, you will probably not wish to go to China (unless, perhaps, you go to Hong Kong or Taiwan). Japan would be a better bet, as would the Philippines, Australia, or New Zealand. We recommend the Southern Hemisphere, in any case, as less liable to fallout in a Soviet-Chinese nuclear war.

At any rate, there may be a possibility for you to escape to less oppressive climes while you can. The Soviets may demand the return of certain people as "war criminals," but lesser figures, especially if they can get false names and papers, may manage.

In your new home, there will inevitably be occasional friction, and you will feel yourself a second-class citizen. Eventually, Communist agents may approach you, pointing to declarations from Soviet Washington promising complete amnesties to émigrés who return. You may be tempted if things are not going well for you. Resist this temptation; except in a few showcases, such promises have always been broken once the returnee is back in Communist hands.

Even after the occupation of America, but especially when five or ten years have passed, you will find your hosts in your new country becoming extraordinarily oblivious to the Soviet threat.

Many will believe Communist propaganda stories about the happy new life in the United States. Others, not quite so naive, will still think there is something in it and feel that you are exaggerating when you tell the true story. Still others (such is the tendency to self-deception found in these circumstances) will believe that it was all or partly America's fault; and that anyhow it cannot be helped. And there will be powerful voices, even among those conducting or discussing foreign policy at a high level, saying that the Soviets are basically reasonable and, if treated with friendship, pose no further threat.

You may say to yourself that they have one excuse: There were people in America who spoke the same way before the disaster.

You will feel it your duty to do what you can to warn your hosts of their own imminent danger. It will not only be a duty, but in your own interest, as the eventual arrival of Soviet troops in your new homeland will be a disaster facing you with no choice but to fight it out to the end, unless you can conceal your origins.

Even so, you will have gained a few years respite—like millions of others throughout the world today. And—who knows? —the interval might just possibly be long enough for the beginning of the inevitable eventual breakup of the Soviet empire to take place first.

When you arrive as a refugee, do not expect too much. However friendly your new host country, it may have no place for your trade or profession not already taken up by one of its present citizens. Be prepared to start again at a low level and work your way up as best you can.

You may even find yourself having to live, as so many millions have in our time, in squalid refugee camps with your whole family in a tent or under a couple of sheets of corrugated iron. Even here, count your blessings; you are a thousand times better off than you would be in the Athabasca labor camps. After the

Russian revolution many émigrés came to Paris. Princes who had lived amidst great privilege became waiters and were glad of the chance.

But in any case, this escape will be open to few.

4

AT HOME

WE THOUGHT IT best to begin with some advice in coping with the more immediate dangers.

However, harder problems will in some ways eventually await those who have not been arrested, or whose arrest is still in the future.

Most people will find that they have to pick themselves up and somehow carry on with their lives. A few, mainly unattached young men, will be able to escape or join the partisan bands, but a family man or a working mother is likely to find that there is no alternative to simply staying put and getting on with their job or with whatever new job they may have been able to get. Fitting into the new order without encountering disaster is going to be a hazardous and wearing experience.

First of all, let us consider the problems that will face you, the ordinary citizen, in your everyday existence. What sort of scene might you expect to see around you as you strive to pick up the after the catastrophe?

Your situation will be squalid for a long time ahead. As

conquerors, the Russians have never shown the slightest inclination to be magnanimous. They will squeeze America dry, and they won't waste any time doing it. We would estimate that in five years, say, after the Occupation, the United States will be shabby, hungry, and cowed. Even that will be an improvement over what it was like immediately after the collapse.

In this connection, it might be instructive for you to acquaint yourself with what was happening in South Vietnam, particularly Saigon, when calamity overwhelmed it. Here was a pro-Western country struck down by a remorseless Soviet-sponsored Communist enemy. The final scenes of defeat might well resemble those that will occur in American cities in the first days. The reconstruction period, with its execution squads and reeducation camps, may bear a close similarity with American events, even allowing for the differences of place, time, and background.

Many of the more prominent features of the new landscape you will inhabit are easy to predict:

- Apart from the purely military destruction, the economy will be thoroughly disrupted.
- Businesses producing anything except the barest necessities will, almost without exception, collapse.
- Oil will no longer be imported. Most domestic American oil will be earmarked for official purposes.
- Nationalization of all major firms will take place almost at Small firms will face the same fate within a year or two.
- Personal savings will be wiped out by the "currency reforms" that will reduce the value of the dollar to one-fiftieth or one-hundredth of the new Red dollar, which alone will be valid thereafter.
- American grain, which has already frequently prevented food within the Soviet Union in past years (shortages brought about by the inefficiency of Soviet agriculture), will be abroad in great quantities. The Russians will take whatever

other foodstuffs they want, and food shortages will result in United States—aggravated by the new agricultural system (see p. 88).

- Large amounts of engineering equipment will be removed to the USSR, often with American technicians attached, as "war reparations" or under some other quasi-legal excuse or will be "purchased" at prices dictated by the Soviets. This would follow the pattern of the dismantling and removal of equipment from Germany and Manchuria in 1945.

One of the first results of Soviet-style "planning" will be an immense expansion of economic bureaucrats and administrators, leading to a corresponding fall off in efficiency. Even the derisory amounts of raw materials that your firm or factory may have been allocated will have been wrongly forecast, and they will never arrive when they are supposed to. Wherever you work, you will encounter severe dislocations and will live in an atmosphere of increasing pressure, corner cutting, faking of results, and so on. The general effects of this on the attitude and morale of you and your fellow workers will be vicious.

Yet there will be a period of brief leeway of which you should take every possible advantage. There will be weeks, even months, during which the occupation forces will be settling down and establishing themselves. The first days will naturally be highly perilous from the point of view of rape, murder, random shootings, and summary executions; but the local commandants will have too many other pressing problems to take over all the stores and smaller businesses immediately. Of course, there will be certain concerns that will peter out at once, such as real estate, others will struggle on with a diminishing stock of goods. The stores alone will be encouraged to keep up their supplies to level and will even be encouraged to replenish their shelves from their contacts in the countryside.

All stores will fall under occupation management as soon as are more or less stabilized. Minor businesses will be supervised official controllers and will require the use of permits for all obtained or sold. Only later will they be formally nationalized and put beneath the umbrella of a new Department of Internal Trade.

Such a vista of businesses that have been wrecked or shut down, or that are functioning only at a fraction of capacity, will somber enough for managers and employees; but it will bear even more heavily on you in your capacity as consumer. So let us at some aspects of the Occupation as they affect you in this most and practical guise.

It is not only privation as such that you will suffer.

Many countries in times of crisis or war have seen their citizens willingly abandon higher standards of living for the national cause. The weekly meat ration in Britain in the 1940s was about the size of a man's thumb and forefinger. American citizens, although not to such a degree, also accepted rationing and shortages and would have been willing to accept far worse if the circumstances had required it.

This time, it will not only be the case that the privations are the result of national humiliation; that much of what you fail to receive, even in basic foodstuffs, will be exported; that an alien-affiliated ruling elite will have far larger rations. What will stick in your throat even more is having every privation you or your family suffer inflicted on you by the decree of those you hate and despise and not even being permitted to grumble about it.

To begin with, the circumstances of the Russian takeover will lead to rigorous rationing. This will continue even after basic foodstuffs cease to be in short supply. Your family will spend a large portion of their time and energies in going around the stores, trying to discover where food and clothing and other necessities are available.

At present, about a third to a half of American women have jobs, but under the Occupation, the number of American women who work will rise until virtually all of them are employed except the very old or the very young—and even a good many of these. Otherwise it will simply not be possible for their families to reach even the minimal prevailing standards of life. Even so, the family food intake will decrease dramatically.

Life, as we have said, will be exceptionally burdensome for many women whose husbands have been arrested. They will often follow them into the camps, their children being taken by the State or boarded out with relatives who are willing and able to have them, as indicated in the last chapter. In the meantime, however, such women will lose their jobs, although they may be able to scrape along by obtaining menial and part-time employment as street cleaners or manual laborers on building sites. Many will beg or scavenge, activities that will be prohibited by the State but that will be so widespread that they will have to be winked at. An additional trial for a woman in this position is that her relatives and friends, to save their own skins, will be forced to shun her and cease to maintain a relationship with her.

But even the ordinary housewife, out shopping, will concentrate on locating supplies of bread and potatoes, which will be the main staples. Meat may be obtained for about one meal a week, if then. Stores will close when their supplies run out and will be virtually mobbed when their doors open. Lines, in which the mood will tend toward a bad temper, will be obligatory not just inside the stores but will commonly stretch along the sidewalk outside and around the corner of the block. Busy mothers will be able to hire the services of elderly people who can earn a few pennies by making a profession of standing or sitting in line as substitutes until the shopper who pays them can get there. Both wives and husbands would also be well-advised to always carry with them a string bag in case they hear of some necessary foodstuff or useful commodity becoming unexpectedly available.

You will not be choosy in the way you shop, and you will take everything on offer. There will not be much of a selection, particularly after present stocks are gone. Normally only one type of soap, stockings, razor and so on will be available. What selection there is will often tend to have an eccentric character. One month the stores will be overflowing with pickled gherkins from Poland or stuffed peppers from East Germany or whatever else the Soviet Union and its partners are dumping on you. Whether or not you and your family are partial to gherkins and peppers, buy them. You may find an imaginative way to serve them up or sell or exchange them with people who like them. It is always a mistake in any Communist country to turn up your nose at any food that happens to be going. The rule is: stock up. And if by any chance you lay your hands on something extra good, keep it for a birthday, an anniversary, a special occasion. It will give you something to look forward to, something memorable to interrupt the wearisome procession of the days.

Above all, make sure you keep your family as well provided as possible with warm clothing. A constant feature of your daily life will be the breakdown of power supplies and other public services. Even when they are restored, fuel shortages and the deterioration of equipment, together with administrative inefficiency, will result in chronic cuts in electricity, gas, and oil, with a ban on all but "essential" uses in the home and elsewhere. Your first winters are liable to be particularly miserable. Central heating, like air-conditioning, will be a thing of the past, except in the districts commandeered by the elite. You would do well to invest in a Swedish-type wood-burning stove and get used to cooking on a Primus stove or some other cooker that works on solid fuel. If you live in the city, it will help you greatly if you have friends or relatives in the country who can help secure you odd items of food. This will depend, of course, on whether the farmers themselves have been left by their overseers with any surplus, or have been clever enough to conceal it. Country friends may also help with good firewood. (In the cities in wintertime, you will notice that the benches, bushes, branches of trees, and even whole trees will mysteriously vanish from the public parks.)

If you live in the suburbs, your lawns and flowerbeds will largely relapse into a natural state since you won't have the time, energy, or gasoline to mow and to tend them, although you may keep a few strips shorn with a hand mower or shears. If you are very lucky, and so situated, it might be possible to use the grass more profitably by keeping chickens and, perhaps, a pig—if you can spare the scraps from your kitchen for nonhuman consumption and can get permission for such activity, as may be the case if you are prepared to let the official concerned have a share of the by-product. All such livestock will even then have to be guarded continuously from sneak thieves and bands of marauders, and this will almost certainly prove very difficult to do. You should consider the risks. For example, it may be possible to keep the pig indoors at night and well watched by day; and neighbors in the same position may collaborate.

You may also be able to grow a few vegetables, although these too will need protection. Fruit trees, if you had them, are likely to have been cut down. But berry bushes of various types may survive and be an invaluable source of vitamins.

You will no longer have a deep freeze and seldom even a refrigerator in working order, but you can bottle or dry out your fruits and vegetables and add them to your store cupboard.

When it comes to purchases, do not rely on food that needs refrigerating since, even if your refrigerator works, the electricity supply will be unreliable, at any rate for some time. Tins and dried foods will be best, as well as being more easily hidden or disguised, and take up less space. But you might explore the possibility of getting hold of one of the old-fashioned iceboxes, which could in the end prove more serviceable and durable than the modern kind.

Speaking of bottles, alcohol will be a tremendous temptation, as it is in all Communist countries. Since, as in all those countries, there will be little in the way of recreation, we do not take it upon ourselves to point out the obvious dangers of lapsing into apathetic soddenness. But be careful how you make home brew—both from the point of view of your health and because it will be illegal and, though usually winked at, be the subject of occasional crackdowns and exemplary sentences to forced labor.

To resume, there are all manner of household items like soap and toothpaste, needle and thread, razor blades, patching materials, flashlight bulbs and batteries, light bulbs and candles, and other odds and ends that seem trivial in time of prosperity but loom large in time of adversity. Sugar, salt, flour, matches, tea, and coffee are other staples that come to mind under this heading, and powdered milk and powdered soups might one day prove especially valuable. These things, if you lay in a stock in time, will help to see you through to when conditions are becoming comparatively better. But the most important items by far will be your reserve of medicines and vitamins. Stock up on these while they are still available and do not stint on them. At a time when sickness and malnutrition will be rife, a couple of aspirin, a cup of beef bouillon, or a spoonful of health-food supplement may save a life. You might also consider getting a quantity of water-purifying tablets.

Tea, coffee, and cigarettes are at a particular premium in the sort of gloomy breakdown that the initial phase of the Occupation will produce. Tea will be of especial value in helping you to carry on, as will coffee, although the demand for the latter will quickly lead to a breakdown in supply, and you may not find palatable the substitutes that will come on the market such as *ersatz* coffee made from acorns.

As for cigarettes, in postwar Europe and Asia they served as the main consolation and stimulant. We do not *urge* you to take up smoking again (one of us is a nonsmoker), but if you do, the risks will be negligible compared with the others facing you. If you do give in to it, you may find the sense of revivification worth it, since unlike other drugs, even alcohol, it will not blunt the edge of your vigilance. Moreover, it will not be discouraged by the

Soviets, and your only real problem will be to obtain tolerable brands. The bulk of American-made cigarettes will be confiscated for use by the Soviet troops and other official bodies, and American tobacco is of such high repute in the USSR that most of the remainder will be exported, at the usual unfavorable trade terms, to Russia and other favored Communist countries. Still, there is such a large amount of tobacco in the United States that it may become, as it did in postwar Europe, a veritable unofficial currency, with a definite exchange value when the dollar itself is collapsing. We would therefore advise you, whether a smoker or not, to gather together a supply and put it to good use during the initial transition period.

With regard to hoarding valuables of other kinds, we would suggest that you forget all about *money*. Dollars will soon be worthless or nearly so. Gold will retain its value, but hoarding of it implies the risk of confiscation and of the labor camp. Nevertheless, as a reserve, and particularly in the case of an attempt to escape to Australia or any other better clime that may still exist, we suggest that a very small, and easily concealed, amount of gold plus a few gemstones of good quality might prove real lifesavers. Gems of great value can look very ordinary and be almost unnoticeable. A mere ounce or two might make all the difference during the process of flight, as has been a common experience in Eastern Europe.

You will also want to have a reserve of more solid property, of a kind not subject to automatic confiscation, that you can sell off from time to time, piece by piece, to help tide you through bad times and to stave off starvation.

These, if you cannot sell or barter privately, you will be able to take to a chain of State-run shops, which will buy the valuables of the ruined "privileged classes" at rates that are a fraction of their real value but that you will have to accept. Here you can dispose of jewelry, silver, pictures, and ornaments.

As for the rest of your possessions, there usually comes a time

71

in any Soviet occupation, usually in the early stages, when most people who own valuable furniture have to sell it off for food or fuel. You should look over your household effects in good time with a view to such an eventuality. Acquire a few more chairs than you need. Choose them in a style that will appeal to the taste of the new rich class of Communist bureaucrats: ornate, pretentious, with some claim to being heirlooms handed down from members of the French aristocracy (or whatever story seems plausible). The proceeds of such a sale may keep you going for weeks or months and may also give you a useful connection with members of the new elite.

All this sounds as if you might need a good deal of space for storage. Above all, be careful to tuck your supplies out of sight not only to save room but to hide them from nosy neighbors who might come poking into your kitchen. They could be the sort of people who, if you quarrel with them (or even if you don't), might denounce you for hoarding. When real shortages develop, anything that might be even mildly stigmatized as "hoarding" will be punishable. Your stores will in any case be liable to confiscation—not automatically, but if local or national authority so decides. We advise you, therefore, to be circumspect in your purchases, not to talk too much about them, and not to look as if you are overdoing your purchasing.

In spite of this need for some caution toward your fellow citizen, we have already implied that you should share your home with other members of your family or invite friends or neighbors to move in. There will be enough of them around whose houses have been confiscated or destroyed. If you don't, the local Communist housing officer, even if he does not confiscate your house, is certain to take over the greater part of it to billet people who will be total strangers and some of whom will be of dubious trustworthiness. Living with people you like, you will be able to share your troubles, bringing up children, doing

72

the shopping, standing in line, and all the day-to-day activities of a problem-packed life. Equally important, you and your new companions may find that one establishment is easier and less costly to run, if you put your minds to it, than two or more, especially in the new circumstances.

The essence of the matter, of course, is compatibility. The fact that people get on each others' nerves at close quarters is nowhere more dramatically illustrated than in the rabbit warrens of Moscow and Leningrad, where a whole underground literature testifies to the neurotic hatreds that flourish. And yet, oddly enough, it is also a fact that people who are capable of behaving toward each other in this churlish fashion will often be found banding together in a crisis and in the face of the State and are capable of touching acts of humble heroism, self-sacrifice, and mutual help. Nevertheless, though especially if you have to receive state-sponsored billeteers, we would advise you to learn a lesson from the apartment dwellers of the Soviet Union and keep everything padlocked, even your pots and pans, and almost literally nail down anything that could possibly be filched.

Needless to say, the household ought also to take pains to stockpile beforehand anything they might need later in the form of tools, nails and screws, shingles, tar for patching holes in the roof, and so on. All these items will become virtually unobtainable after the war when present stocks are exhausted, as they will be very low on the list of objects that the occupation authorities will ordain for manufacture.

A good set of ladders (padlocked) will be useful as well as several sheets of glass. It is demoralizing to have to live in a house whose windows are broken or boarded up with plywood or cardboard, and being able to mend your smashed windows will give you a small psychological lift. On the other hand, it will not be advisable to paint the exterior of your house or lavish too much care and attention on it. See that it is sound- and waterproof, but otherwise foster a discreet shabbiness. You won't want your house to stand out. Begin to cultivate early the art of keeping a low profile.

There will be work enough inside the house to keep you going. You will have endless trouble with your plumbing. In general, we would strongly urge both men and women to become do-it-yourself experts. Develop, as far as possible, any skills you may have in the fields of maintenance and repair. This will not only be useful at home but marketable in the world outside. It could provide you with a small steady income and serve as one of the other jobs that you will have to do if you are to make ends meet. Except for the elite, plumbers, carpenters, and electricians will be hard to come by. (Such skills may also save your life if you land in a labor camp.) Try to obtain a sewing machine—hand or foot, not electrically, operated. You will then be equipped, at some time in the future, to earn extra money for the family as a seamstress, dressmaker, or even an upholsterer.

There are many automobiles in America. Few will be left in "private" hands, except for those allocated to the Party and the Russians. Most will be pulled into car pools run by the offices and enterprises; here too, the more privileged people will have first choice. (There will be a limited number of jobs as drivers in both these categories, and you may be able to get one. However, in spite of advantages such as occasional tips or food from the Party bosses, you may prefer not to have your life disrupted by irregular hours, to say nothing of the risk of failing to keep the car in good repair for want of spare parts and facing a charge of sabotage.) But in any case, the shortage of gasoline will drive the majority of cars off the road, and unless you can get a special ration, as may be possible for distant farmers, you are unlikely to be able to use your own car, even if you can keep it.

Mobile caravans will be confiscated, unless you must live in yours yourself if your home is appropriated or destroyed. Yachts and powerboats will be compulsorily laid up or put out of action. If you possess a seagoing vessel you might, of course, think about using it while you can, during or immediately after the cessation of hostilities, to try to make a run for freedom. Such a course of action obviously requires a good deal of reflection and planning.

The preferred, indeed almost the only, mode of private transport will be the bicycle. You might like to be prepared by buying yourself and the other members of your family good sturdy no-nonsense vehicles while the supply is still plentiful and while you can lay in a stock of tires and accessories. Don't buy bicycles that are too flimsy and too flashy and that are likely to attract disapproving or dishonest eyes. Paint the chrome gray or black or otherwise dull it over. Get a strong padlock. You may find that you have to bicycle a long way to your place of work and back, with perhaps a good many hills and obstacles besides; but except in bad weather, you might find that this acts as something of a tonic since it will enable you to work off the side effects of your often starchy diet while providing you with moderate exercise at the same time.

After some weeks, a public transport system in the form of buses, and eventually subways, will be reestablished, at least in a skeletal form. The railways will survive, probably burning coal since coal is plentiful in the United States and the mines (strikes being forbidden) will be one of the few industries working to full capacity. And it may be that you will become accustomed to seeing on the streets of America those weird and ingenious contraptions that circulated in Europe in World War II.

5

THE INDIVIDUAL
BY PROFESSION,
OPINION, AND HABIT

WE HAVE GIVEN YOU something of the general picture of what your life, as an American, will be like under Soviet rule—and we shall be giving you more in later chapters. But you will also be anxious to know how someone of your own particular professional and ethnic and political and tempermental background is likely to fare. In the pages that follow, we look into the special conditions facing a wide variety of these, of a reasonably representative nature, from Academic to Farmer, from Realtor to Industrial Worker, from Black to Student, from Homosexual to Feminist, from Soldier to Traitor.

Academic

When universities reopen after the crisis, student numbers will have gone down. Some will be dead, some in prison, some in the partisan movement.

Private, religious, and racially or ethnically oriented institutions will have been taken over by the State. All departments, but especially those of history, philosophy, political science, economics, and sociology, will be purged of "incorrect" teachers with great thoroughness. The curricula will be thinned down and streamlined along Russian lines, with the more controversial and enterprising elective courses omitted.

Colleges will be run by Communist-appointed functionaries, including representatives of the secret police, and there will be no "academic freedom." If you are at the moment an academic with Communist or Marxist leanings, you can expect to become at least a dean or the head of your department, at least for as long as your orthodoxy is regarded as adequate. If you lack such credentials, you must make up your mind to tread warily and keep your mouth shut. Eschew the banter, gossip, and small talk that is normally the small change of academic life. Departmental infighting will cease to be a diversion and will become a blood-sport, the losers being consigned to the ranks of bricklayers, coal miners, and washroom attendants, if lucky. Sneaking and denunciation will be the order of the day, and since the arrest rate will be one of the highest in any field, you will be hard put to trust your colleagues, for you will not be able to tell which of them have become police informers, either of their own volition or through blackmail.

Similarly, take care not to make unguarded remarks to your students since one or more of the students in each of your classes will be stool pigeons or undercover "observers," or starry-eyed members of the Party. Be generous with your grades since disgruntled students will denounce you, and if convenient, their complaints will be produced as hard evidence of your unreliability.

On the other hand, some professors may be relieved to find that the student body will otherwise become hardworking, respectful, and serious to the point of being subdued (see *Student* below). Campus protests will be a thing of the past.

You will find giving and attending Marxism-Leninism classes boring, but if you can manage to appear enthusiastic you will be rewarded accordingly. The hardest thing to which you will have to accustom yourself will be the distortion of your researches and of scholarship in general. Many of the books that you will need to consult will have been removed from the shelves of the library; and your own articles, theses, and books will be subject to State censorship. Publishing outlets will in any case be few and themselves under State control (see *Publisher*). You will find it necessary to import Marxist-Leninist jargon into the most unlikely topics, and it will take you some years to acquire the ability that academics in the older Communist countries have developed of discounting the obligatory Party-line nonsense and reading between the lines. At first, the necessity of accepting and expressing ideas that are mendacious, silly, or downright crackpot will depress you; in time you may get used to it. (See also *Schoolteacher; Scientist.*)

Accountant

If deemed suitable, you will be incorporated into the burgeoning government apparatus at a flat salary.

Actor

Theatrical enterprises and the entertainment industry will come under the control of government administrators and will be severely curtailed. Productions of plays and films will be cut back and their predominant style will be stereotyped and will adhere to the dogma of "socialist realism" (see *Artist; Writer*). Censorship will be strict, and comedy and "satire" will be bland to the point of toothlessness. The repertoire will be meager and restricted to safe and unexceptionable material. Theatrical people, even more than academics (see above), are given to indiscretion, love gossip, and say what they feel like saying at the moment when they feel like saying it. Break yourself of this habit. Keep your grievances and your witticisms to yourself. This will not be easy since you will see the plum roles going to mediocre performers who happen to be members of the Party or who stand well with it. But you must persevere.

Advertising Agency Owner or Employee

This class of work will be terminated.

Aircraft Manufacturer or Worker

Aircraft factories will be nationalized, drastically reduced in scale, and subject to exceptionally stringent security controls. Key technicians may be dispatched to the USSR. (See also *Scientist; Industrial Worker*).

Air Force (see Military)

Alcoholic

Officially, drinking will be discouraged, but the State will need its large income from taxes on liquor, so alcohol will be easy enough to obtain. Quality, as in the case of most other consumer goods, will be sacrificed to quantity, and those better brands that survive will be available only at great cost and to privileged purchasers. Home brews will be much cheaper and more potable than most State products, so there will be a great proliferation in illicit distilling. Heavy drinking and drunkenness will sharply increase. Partly, as in the Soviet Union and other Communist countries, this will be the result of the general unpleasantness of life; partly it will be because of the dearth of other forms of entertainment.

Although drunkenness will be more or less tolerated, since drinkers seldom become politically troublesome, alcoholism leading to persistent lateness or trouble on the job or to rowdy behavior in public will not. For the drunks who are found littering the streets, there will be the kind of rugged drying-up centers and sobering-up tanks that exist at the present time in Soviet cities, where the offender is dehydrated, deloused, made to go "cold turkey," and not released until detoxicated.

Anarchist

You will be shot or sent to a labor camp quicker than most.

Antique Dealer

Your premises will be looted more efficiently and less crudely than most by men sent by senior Russian officers to skim off the cream of your stock. If you work in a small way and maintain your shop in a shabby and unobtrusive condition, you may be allowed to continue on a reduced scale, as you can serve as a point where Americans can bring their remaining small treasures that you will then resell on commission to the occupiers.

Architect

No new buildings will be erected for some time. You may obtain work on rebuilding and repairs. Eventually, buildings will be constructed according to Soviet principle. Take care to avoid all styles that are original, "modern," and imaginative and stick to the concrete-box type of architecture. You will be a government employee, on a fixed salary, with occasional bonuses for acceptable service.

Army (see Military)

Artist

Styles differing in any marked degree from "socialist realism" will not receive permission to be exhibited. Socialist Realism is a form of Victorian academic painting and sculpture used to point up morals acceptable to and glorifying the State and the Communist leadership. The style was instituted by Stalin in 1934 when he officially decreed that art must be "the truthful depiction of reality in its revolutionary development." By "truthful," Stalin meant Communist in content and photographic in form. For half a century Soviet art has been frozen in this vulgar and stodgy posture. After the Occupation, American artists will also be required to adhere to the tradition of Soviet art and will find it safer and more profitable to abandon all thought of being adventurous and experimental.

On the other hand, employment will be readily available in the mass production of propaganda posters, crude cartoons, and the illustration of Party literature. There will be a continuous demand for portraits, statues, and murals depicting those political figures who are in good odor, although if you are commissioned to execute such set pieces of the Communist leadership, you should, if possible, design them in such a way that the figures of those members of the original cast who have fallen into disfavor can easily be erased at a later date.

General instructions as to style and content will be issued regularly by the science and culture department of the Central Committee of the Communist party, so there will be no actual need for an artist to worry about giving offense as long as he follows the simple official pronouncements. However, artists ambitious for more than average success and remuneration will be well-advised to keep abreast of political developments. Still, caution is needed, and it is not advisable to attach yourself too closely to any single patron, who might suddenly disappear in a reshuffle.

If you receive your diploma after four years at an official art school, you will be registered as a member of the Union of Artists. With your diploma, you will be ipso facto "an artist." Without it, you will not be able to join the union and so will never be eligible to exhibit in any museum or gallery or in any of the officially sponsored art exhibits; as an artist, you will be a lifelong "nonperson." If you wish, you can work on your own, without much fear of actual arrest, at least for this reason, although you can only put up your pictures on the walls of your own apartment, where people will be cautious about coming to see them and more cautious still about expressing an opinion about them.

If you are fortunate enough to become a member of the union, we would advise you, unless you are a born intriguer, not to become too deeply involved with its caucuses and committees. Artists who emerge on the wrong side are liable to denunciation and expulsion, with the consequent end of their careers.

Athlete

At first there will be a great decline in the number of teams since resources will be lacking. The whole sphere of sports will be brought under Party control. Then, selected teams will be fostered in all the main games. Thus, the professional athlete temporarily out of a job in his speciality and confident of his skill should stay in training as long as he can in the hope of returning.

Professionalism will be unknown in theory, but in practice athletes will be given office and other jobs at which they will not be required to work, so that they will be professional in fact if not in name. But the teams will be sponsored by the bodies supposedly employing them—that is, by various bureaucratic and party institutions. The secret police has always been prominent among these in Communist countries, and some athletes may not wish to work, even in this indirect way, for such a body— even apart from the fact that the police team is naturally always the most unpopular with the fans. On the other hand, if you are good, transfer to a secret police team may be hard to avoid.

Once accepted for a team or for track events, the athlete will do comparatively well as far as rations and perquisites are concerned; but he will have no rights with his employers. And, however popular, he is liable to be made an example of to deter others. Thus, the three Starostin brothers, soccer stars under Stalin, were sent to labor camps. And in Czechoslovakia, the great national athlete Zatopek was stripped of all his positions and given menial work when he supported popular resistance to the USSR.

Games played against "fraternal" teams from Moscow will sometimes be the occasion of "anti-Soviet demonstrations" by American fans; and the players will not escape blame.

All the same, the dangers of the profession are comparatively small, and you will have the satisfaction of being able to give your fellow citizens harmless pleasure at a time when there will be little of that around.

Automobile Dealer

Out of business.

Banker or Bank Employee

Banks will be among the first businesses to be nationalized. Services will be cut to the barest minimum—indeed, even checking accounts are regarded with suspicion by the Soviets. Savings will be limited to State bonds, although there will be little spare money to save. Credit cards will be abolished. (See also *Businessperson.*)

Barber

Barber shops will be countenanced, although any but the most orthodox haircuts will be heavily discouraged. You may not be nationalized for several years but will then become standardized and paid as a public servant, under a new Department of Internal Trade, as in other Communist countries.

Beautician

Most beauty salons will close for lack of patrons with enough money to be able to afford such luxuries. A few will remain open at the center of big cities to serve the new Communist elite and the wives of Soviet generals and senior officers.

Black

It has always been a Communist aim to penetrate and control black movements in the United States, with a view, first of all, to using them against the American system, and second, to persuading them that only under communism can the black get justice. The Russians will turn their attention to the blacks, as to the other minorities, as a major article of policy. Black Commu-

87

nists will at first enjoy a disproportionate chance of being given a high position. On the other hand, the importance attached by the Russians to building up black participation and cooperation in the political sphere is going to result in particularly strict purges of those black leaders and organizations that stand in the way of such plans. Those that emphasize the idea of a black culture different from the official one and unassimilable to it, such as the Black Muslims, will be crushed at once. Others will simply be placed under black Communist leaders; and these in turn will suffer the usual cycle of purges. Such groups as compete for the souls of the black population, like the Southern Baptists, will be taken over, or disrupted, with special ruthlessness as the Soviets seek to capture the black constituency.

For the unpolitical majority of blacks, the Occupation is bound to bring about a sudden turn for the worse. While equality of the races as well as of the sexes (see *Feminist* below) will have been proclaimed, there will be a cessation of all quotas in jobs and education and a cancellation of all "equal opportunity" and "affirmative action" programs. There will no longer be a problem of black unemployment—in the sense that people who are unemployed cannot expect to have their problems more or less sympathetically examined at their labor exchanges, but instead will be summarily directed into any kind of job or into the regular labor corps or labor battalions.

The American Communists at one time envisaged a black Soviet republic in the old "Black Belt" in the South; but this was abandoned long ago in favor of an integrationist attitude, and it now seems unlikely, although perhaps not quite impossible, that it will be revived. More probably areas with a high proportion of black population will have black mayors, and the first secretary of the local Communist party will also be black. But it is a principle of the Soviet order that the interests of the Party come first, and that key power positions must be filled according to this principle regardless of racial or other considerations. The Soviet method is to give all powers of controlling personnel to the *second* secretary, who, in minority areas in the Soviet Union, is almost invariably a white man appointed directly from the Central party apparatus. You will often find, in fact, that a rather shadowy figure from out of state, often white, will be the repository of real power in your neighborhood. It will be an offense for black party members to raise the issue and will result in their removal.

It will be declared that complete equality now reigns and much publicity will be given to figures proving that this is so. No independent bodies will exist to investigate or question these figures or to draw attention to spheres which have been mysteriously left unrecorded. If you do discover imbalances, you will not be in a position to launch a campaign about them unless it is a very short one cut off abruptly by arrest.

Thus in the earlier phase, the Soviets will need to strengthen their position as best they can, and in the face of sullen distaste for the new order, they will seek to use the minorities. In the long run, however, and as they entrench themselves, they will begin to place emphasis on the majority.

The Russian record with their own minorities is, indeed, very bad. In theory all nations are equal, but in practice control by Russians, the Russification of schools, and the repression of all nationalist elements is continual. In Stalin's time eight small nations, totaling about a million and a half people, were deported—every man, woman, and child—from their homelands to Siberia and central Asia, where around a third of them died. To this day, although the charges against them have been dropped, three of these nations, numbering about half a million, are still in exile.

Bookstore Owner or Employee

Bookstores will be State-run and will only stock State-printed literature. Employment may possibly be obtained in one of the

89

State stores, though your previous exposure to non-Communist books will render you suspect. (See also *Librarian; Publisher.*)

Building Contractor

You will be regarded as a virtually unreconstructible member of the bourgeoisie, and your chances of remaining at liberty are low. In any case your firm will at once be incorporated in the new Department of Construction and your workers will become low-grade state employees. (See also *Contractor.*)

Businessperson

Big-time businesspeople, and particularly such paladins of capitalism as bankers and stockbrokers, will almost all be arrested and sent to the labor camps. Later, a few with specialist abilities may be released, if they have survived, and put to work in the State monopolies.

On the other hand, if you are in a small business and have not given offense in other respects, you may be allowed to go on operating during an interim period. Be prepared to accept detailed instructions as to how to proceed. Raw materials and their distribution will be under central control from the outset, as we indicated earlier, and they will be in short supply; but failure to fulfill your quota and meet your obligations will not be excused on the grounds that you could not obtain your raw materials through legal channels. Unfortunately, if you are enterprising enough to obtain them illegally or on the black market, that will not be condoned either. You will be between a rock and a hard place. Moreover the taxation on your profits, if any, will be extortionate and will change in a capricious fashion. Your operations will be further hampered by the fact that a "representative" of your employees (really a nominee of the Party) will have the power to oversee all your activities.

Once the transition is over, your business will revert to the State. If you accept this in what your bosses would regard as a constructive manner, there is a faint chance that you might be retained as a manager on a lower level, although it is more likely that you will be transferred to some job in the local economic administration. There it is not impossible that you might be able to work obscurely for a number of years until such time as one of the new generation of Party-trained administrators is ready to take over. Even then, if you become a model of obedience, you might manage to become a janitor or junior clerk in some institution or even be given a small pension.

Whatever happens to you, your class origins will have been recorded on your identity documents and will remain a stigma for the rest of your life. Your children, because of their own class origins, will in all cases be denied equal opportunity in education, in obtaining jobs, and in all other walks of life.

Chicano, Mexican, Spanish American

As in the case of the blacks, the Communists will make every effort, particularly in the earlier days of the Occupation, to harness Chicano aspirations in their own interests.

And, as with blacks, all Chicano organizations will be taken over by Communist appointees, and any who resist this will be disposed of.

There seems to be a real possibility that the Communists—whose administrative principle in the USSR and elsewhere has been a linguistic one—might eventually create a Chicano autonomous area in the Spanish-speaking borderlands or even erect a new state (or possibly cede a strip of territory to a new Soviet Mexico). On the other hand, recent Soviet policy has tended away from such arrangements in favor of giving a preponderant role to economic and administrative factors. Moreover, for a considerable time the idea of leaving America looking on the surface as it always was and thus giving the majority a stable and "patriotic" impression will weigh heavily. In principle, although using lesser nationalisms as weapons in the struggle for power, the Communists rely basically, where they can, on the large industrial state. They will seek to make the United States their main bastion on the continent, basing themselves as far as possible in the majority section.

Different communities will in any case receive different treatment. For instance, the Spanish-speaking community of Florida, with its high proportion of anti-Castro refugees from Cuba, will suffer probably more than any other section of the United States' population. Their mass transfer back to Cuba as forced laborers, after the execution of the more notable anti-Communist figures, will be automatic unless Castro, or his successor, prefers to leave them to disposition by the Soviet-American secret police, in which case few will escape the Arctic labor camps.

Illegal immigration will cease. Border controls, even between Communist states, are very strict. (And when people cannot move even within their own country without identity documents, and they have to register with the police when outside their hometown, movement will in any case be difficult.) Indeed, depending on their judgment of economic and political needs, it seems probable that the Soviet authorities will initiate a repatriation program for any Chicano labor they regard as surplus.

A Sovietized America will anyhow not be much of an attraction for the poor even of Sovietized Mexico or Colombia.

Chinese American

All Chinese Americans will be automatically suspect. This will apply whether they have shown any sympathy toward the Chinese People's Republic or to its rivals on Taiwan or whether they have been completely apolitical. If China has still to be overrun by the Soviet Union, they will be regarded as potentially active partisans of the enemy and will be deported from such sensitive areas as the Pacific Coast. Even if and when China has been conquered, they will continue to be looked on as inherently untrustworthy and will be subject to a higher rate of arrest than the ordinary population.

Civil Servant

Russians have always been dedicated pen pushers, and like all inefficient social systems, the Soviet Union is a bureaucrats' paradise. There will be no lack of reports to compile and forms to fill in, with a corresponding need for hordes of clerks. Senior civil servants will have been removed, but if you are a junior officer in a noncontroversial department, if you stay at your desk, don't argue with your superiors, and keep your eyes on your work, you will have a good chance of keeping your job until younger and better-oriented people can be produced. Millions of posts of sorts in the civil service, and in the even more greatly enlarged local administrations, will become available for those thrown out of work by the cessation of various productive enterprises. Real wages will be low, but little real work will be required.

Clergyman

All churches will be registered. They will come under the leadership of officially approved boards responsible to the Religious Affairs Office of the government. A selection of pro-Communist clergy of each denomination will be solicited as members of "peace" committees and other similar bodies. Government policy towards the churches will vary. There will be periods, particularly in the early days, when church leaders who are reluctant to submit to official control will be arrested and subjected to public "trials," after which they will be sent to prison or a labor camp. Local clergy will also be liable to mass arrest.

It will be general policy to close down as many churches, seminaries, and theological colleges as possible, while leaving enough to justify the assertion that religious liberty is not being infringed. Large sums and spacious premises will be given to the League of Militant Atheists; antireligious museums will be opened in the main cities; and courses of atheist lectures will be given throughout the country on Lenin's principle that: "Every religious idea, every idea of God, even flirting with the idea of God, is unutterable vileness."

It will be illegal to teach children a religious faith. This will be hard to enforce on a family basis, but priests and rabbis who feel it their duty to teach children religion will be arrested when caught.

A few minor religious groups, including the Jehovah's Witnesses and the Ukrainian Uniates, will be totally suppressed; and others, including the Mormons and Christian Scientists, will be treated with notable rigor.

The Jewish religion will suffer severely; only a few synagogues will remain open, the Hebrew scriptures will be hard to obtain, and pressure will be brought to prevent the baking of matzohs. Many rabbis will be arrested on trumped-up charges of black market activity.

Baptists will also be peculiarly ill regarded by the Communist authorities since, although they will have imposed on them an official leadership appointed by the State, it has been found that everywhere in Eastern Europe and the Soviet Union—and the same will presumably happen in America—they reject such leadership and tend to set up illegal or semi-illegal structures of their own. The Russian answer will be mass arrests, but even so they will be unable to root out the movement entirely.

The choice for the clergy of other religious bodies is either to return to the catacombs or to try to reach an accord with the State to leave them at least a few seminaries and churches. They will then have to devote much time to keeping as much control as possible out of the hands of agents intruded by the State. Church leaders taking this option will face a hard and continuous balancing act and many problems of conscience.

Perhaps we should note that, in spite of the hostility of communism to religion as such, there have always been a small proportion of clergy willing to support communism. Some of them do so out of venality or from a perverted idealism. Such "people's priests" are flattered and accorded a high ration scale and are well looked after. Unfortunately for themselves and for the cause that they have elected to serve, they are despised by everyone, including the Communists themselves.

Finally, may we say that members of all denominations may draw strength and encouragement from the fact that communism, in spite of titanic efforts, has nowhere proved effective in extirpating religious faith. Indeed, there are many cases of heroic clergy-and laymen surviving successive sentences in the labor camps, where they brought hope and succor to their fellow inmates, and have remained inspirational figures to their flocks and fellow worshipers.

Communist

Your immediate future is bright. Whatever your field, you will find yourself elevated to a leading position. The small size of the

Party need not worry you. In central and Eastern Europe, particularly in Romania and the Baltic states, Communist parties that had no more than a few hundred members were rapidly expanded into organizations capable of ruling the entire country. However, during the first period, members will have to be recruited or retained in the Party without too much regard for their moral or ideological suitability, so you will need to get used to working at close quarters with the careerists, psychopaths, and other dubious characters who have been accepted in order to swell the membership of your organization. Nevertheless, within it, you and your fellow veterans will remain the directing element.

On the other hand, this can prove a doubtful privilege as experience shows that such "old Communists" are never entirely fit to be the perfect bearers of the Russian will. Some of you will turn out to have been hopelessly infected by the non-Communist atmosphere of the pre-Soviet United States. Others among you will discover that the new order does not conform to the enthusiastic expectations you had formed, while still others of you will find yourselves resenting having to take orders from Russians and increasingly unable to conceal it. Some of you may let this become apparent, when it will be necessary to purge you from the Party; in which event your prospects will become precarious indeed. Communists who have found themselves in opposition to the Soviet-supported leadership may anticipate prison, at best, and often torture, the confession of their crimes, and execution. Others will keep quiet and carry on without any heart for it. In many cases it is found that these gradually become hardened, until they cease to listen to the internal voice of conscience or even of experience. Indeed, those who put a foot wrong once, and teeter on the brink of arrest but are given another chance, have often turned out to be the very worst of the new ruling class trying desperately to prove their loyalty. Even this will seldom save you in the long run.

Contractor

The whole principle of "contracting" is contrary to Communist theory. You will be nationalized and competition will cease, together with profits and adequate wages.

Criminal

The conditions of shortage that will prevail for many years will offer continuous opportunities for the individual criminal and for localized crime rings. The authorities will be too preoccupied with political offenders to give much time to ordinary wrong-doers. On the other hand, if mugging or theft become unduly obnoxious in a given area, they will be suppressed by police firing squads. And there will be periodic crackdowns on the major black-market operations.

Criminals sentenced and sent to forced-labor camps will, as we saw in an earlier chapter, receive better treatment than political prisoners. They will be encouraged by the guards to become gang bosses and to beat and bully prisoners who are stigmatized as "enemies of the people." They will enjoy softer working conditions and may be able to divert the bulk of the camp rations to their own use, to consume or to use as currency.

Dentist

The level of dental care in the population will fall. Especially during the first few months, dental stocks will dwindle and dental equipment will deteriorate for lack of spare parts and specialized servicing. Dental techniques will become basic, with extraction taking precedence over filling. Dentures will be poorly made and ill fitting when available. At times extractions

97

will have to be performed without anesthetic because of the absence of supply. Many dentists will give up in despair or because they cannot accede to the decline in professional standards. Receptionists, nurses, and dental technicians will, in general, become a thing of the past, and as well as accustoming themselves to carrying on their businesses single-handedly, dentists should be willing to contemplate receiving payment in kind rather than cash. Those dentists who have acquired as a curiosity, or have perhaps inherited, one of the old-fashioned treadle-operated drills might consider taking it out and dusting it off, since in times of electricity failures and shortage of spare parts, it might prove more reliable than more up-to-date models.

None of the above will apply to dental specialists with a clientele among the elite and the senior occupation officials.

Eventually the entire profession will be incorporated into a Soviet-style health service as government employees.

Doctor

Many doctors will be regarded, for political and class reasons, as enemies of the people. But the Communist State will stand in urgent need of the medical profession since, even if the takeover of the United States were to prove unexpectedly peaceful, the disruption of public services will soon lead to epidemics on a large scale. As the levels of nutrition sink, the health of the population will further decline. Doctors who survive will therefore be in a comparatively favorable position; and those who are outstanding specialists will thrive even more because their services will be in demand by members of the Communist hierarchy itself, either in Washington or in Moscow and Leningrad.

That is not to say that such medical specialists should not adopt certain precautions. If rival schools spring up over aspects of medical treatment or biological theory, the leading proponents of the vanquished school will pay the price. Do not commit yourself too firmly. Leading specialists must also be warned that if they treat political notables, it can be very dangerous if their patients die on their hands.

It has happened twice in the Soviet Union that whole groups of doctors in this situation have been given particularly bad treatment at the hands of the secret police as "murderers in white coats."

Doctors in a more humdrum way of business should read the entry *Dentist* above. In time, of course, all doctors will become State employees; and hospitals and clinics will be Communist-run, which will entail an increase in employees and a decrease in effectiveness. Though private practice will not be illegal, it should be conducted with the utmost care. Watch out for dissatisfied or neurotic patients who may denounce you. When in his sixties, Russia's leading heart specialist was jailed on a fake charge of assaulting a patient, to give the secret police the opportunity to soften him up for more serious accusations.

Dressmaker

Existence will be extremely difficult at first; but eventually people will need to squeeze a longer life out of their old clothes or will need to get them cut down for younger members of the family. Those who do not possess, or cannot master, the necessary skills will turn to you. Be prepared to offer to mend curtains and perhaps develop a sideline with the lighter types of upholstery. It will be a hand-to-mouth existence, but when all shops have become nationalized you may have a chance of being taken on as a government employee. If not, it may still be possible for you to eke out a living in a private capacity, in conjunction with a sister or daughter, from your own house or apartment or, rather, room.

Drugtaker

At first, drug addicts and drug dealers will probably be shot. Later, they will receive the current Soviet sentence of five years for possession of drugs, including marijuana, and ten years for pushing or influencing other people to take drugs. These sentences are served in labor camps.

Eastern European American

The Russians will probably mete out severer treatment to Americans who are of Eastern European stock than to those whose forebears came from Western Europe. The reason is simple: Poland, Hungary, Romania, Bulgaria, and Yugoslavia are close to the Soviet Union, and most Americans migrating from those countries are well informed about Soviet imperialism. American citizens of Eastern European origin who can be identified as in any way anti-Soviet will be among the first to be pushed into the cattle trucks.

On the other hand, the Russians will, as with other groups, want to utilize the American Poles, the American Hungarians, and the rest in an active fashion, to further their own aims. All their organizations will be brought under control, and there will be a great expansion of the existing "friendship societies" with the Eastern European countries.

Ecologist, Environmentalist

You must remember that the plan will impose on the Party secretary of your State, and his subordinate the governor, the maximum they can cope with. To fulfill a timber plan (for example) they will have to make irreplaceable inroads into the forests. After all, the next year they may receive a transfer or promotion and it will be their successor who is blamed for any

100

later shortfall. Similar considerations apply to pollution, which has produced a stinking morass to accompany the hydroelectric developments on the Volga, lifeless stretches on the Caspian and Lake Baikal, and the erosion of the ancient statues of Prague by lignite fumes.

The Party and government in the USSR and other Communist countries do not intend these results, even though production always comes first. If you can assemble a small group of scientists who are politically impeccable, they may be allowed to make representations about particularly horrible offenses to the environment, and in some cases, improvement will be effected—especially if it can be shown that the pollution has a long-term ill effect on productivity. But no public organization, demonstration, or other activity will, of course, be permitted. As for nuclear power stations (under strict Soviet control for reasons of military security), they will be developed to the limit. No sort of objection to them will be permitted in any circumstances.

However, there will be one area in which improvement will have been made: the shortage of private cars will mean less pollution from gasoline.

Economist

"Bourgeois" economics will, in principle, be a banned subject. If you have been prominent in any of the fields covered by this term, and in particular if you have justified the free-market system, you have no professional future and had best seek a job in accountancy. If you have worked on purely quantitive matters, and are prepared to give the appearance of accepting the set of abstract dogmas called Marxist economics, you may well find employment (probably under Soviet advisers) in one of the agencies of the new State Planning Committee.

One of your problems will be that many of the statistics you will need to work with are either unavailable or falsified—as with the present Soviet method of estimating grain yields, which exaggerates them by an estimated 20 percent.

You will find that even your Soviet colleagues would wish the government to use genuinely economic methods but that they have mostly given up hope that anything but purely administrative methods of compulsion will be allowed. We advise you to remain discreet in any discussion of this.

Engineer or Technician

You will be in great demand. Nonetheless, because of your "class" origin, you will not be regarded as wholly trustworthy, so you will be under rather strict supervision. Some of you will be compelled to "volunteer" to go to the USSR to operate the American machinery that has been taken there and to instruct Soviet technicians in its use. You will be paid well by Soviet standards, but you should prepare yourself for a different style of life.

However, most of you will be employed in developing American industry under the new system, and since that system is inefficient and yet exerts grinding pressure on all concerned, in it you will find yourself at constant risk. For example, in a desperate effort to meet unrealistic quotas, directors will have no choice but to relax or abandon safety standards, which will result in disasters. For every type of shortcoming the "bourgeois" engineer is the natural scapegoat and will figure prominently in trials for "sabotage."

We therefore suggest that senior engineers and technicians should try to gain employment in enterprises where raw materials are in fairly regular supply and where safety factors are not paramount. Where possible, you should stick to the development rather than the production side of industry and, whenever you can, get any instructions that look as if they might lead to trouble in writing, make two copies, and keep a copy at home. If the enterprise that you direct or in which you are a prominent figure seems likely to land you in danger, you will not be allowed to resign without permission; but by keeping your eyes open early enough, you may conceivably be able to escape in time by finding some other plant that will request a transfer for you. Your main danger, apart from these, will raise its head in ten of fifteen years' time, when the new dispensation will have trained enough indoctrinated Communists to take over management. (See also *Businessperson* above.)

Farmer

If you are a big farmer, your farm will be immediately confiscated and will be run by a Communist official who will be sent to direct it. Your class status will probably entail arrest, although in certain cases you may be allowed, for a time, to work on your former land as an employee. In general, if you have been a successful farmer, even if on a small scale, and particularly if you have employed hired labor, you will be labeled a "kulak" and be subject to deportation. Even if you survive deportation and return to civil life, you will carry the "class" label on your identity documents and remain under a permanent stigma. Your children will be discriminated against with regard to education and jobs.

If you are a farmer on an extremely modest scale, with no hired help, you may at first be rather better treated; and if there are any large landholdings in your neighborhood, you may be given part of them for the time being. However if, as is likely, during the first months and years of the Occupation there are drastic food shortages, you will be required to hand over everything you produce to the State agencies, from whom you will get back whatever they think fit. If the shortages are particularly grave, your crop may be taken without any compensation whatever since it will be regarded as more important to feed the towns than to feed the countryside.

Then, if conditions improve, you may for a while be allowed more latitude and be permitted to sell your produce, under supervision, at something approaching regular market prices.

Thus, even the small farmer is going to be faced with many ticklish problems, of which the plummeting of his standard of living will be the simplest. In fact, it is going to be virtually impossible for the rural population to function at all without making at least some sales (and purchases) through the black market. Official reaction to this is going to be bewilderingly erratic and capricious. Sometimes a local commissar, anxious to save his own skin, will crack down at random on any farmer he catches or suspects. At other times, when he is not under pressure himself and is eager to keep the quotas of his own district respectable, he may decide to turn a blind eye. Orders from the center, too, will vary. Sometimes the need for productivity will take priority and the farmer can breathe fairly freely; but this policy may be abruptly and arbitrarily reversed, and the call will go out for tighter control. If you are a small farmer, we can only tell you to keep your eyes open for these developments and trim your conduct accordingly.

On past form, you should remember that, once the 20-30 percent of the adult population who are suspect for other reasons have been dealt with, it is always the farmer who is the first victim of mass operations against society in general. Sooner or later, the Russians always impose their own system of farming. In some cases, there has been no intermediate period at all, and collectivization has been introduced at once without any pre-liminary phase. In America, it is almost certain that a more gradual approach will be attempted. In any event, after a longer or shorter interim, many small farmers will in turn be declared kulaks and deported to the Arctic, while the rest will be ordered to merge their farms with those of their twenty or thirty nearest neighbors. If you are among these, you will be permitted to keep an acre or two and a few animals in your own name. The rest will cease to be your property, and you will work your "collective farm" with your neighbors under a Communist-appointed director sent in from the city. No later than the time of the collectivization, the system of identity cards will be transformed into a system of internal passports, whereupon the rural population will be discouraged from leaving the countryside by being forbidden to visit even the local town for periods of more than five or six days.

The individual's chance of arrest and deportation during the actual collectivization campaign is perhaps one in eight, higher in the case of farmers in prosperous areas.

Feminist

Full equality of both sexes will be officially decreed. However, no "affirmative action" in the case of women or any other section of the community will be taken or permitted, and you will be expected not to voice any complaints you may have in this regard. No attempt will be made to secure female participation in any job through quotas, and in practice very few women will attain positions or high-salary brackets within their profession. In Communist countries, women traditionally predominate in teaching and the lower ranks of the medical profession and are prominent in manual labor in the cities and particularly on the farms but rarely attain important political or professional status.

Present-day feminist organizations will be wound up, but a women's organization under Communist supervision will be set up, with the main object of establishing "friendly relations" with their Russian women's counterpart and the preaching of "peaceful reconciliation." Posts in it will be available to American women with organizational experience, especially those now prominent in pro-Soviet women's bodies. It might also be noted that mass arrests will have removed more men than women, in the proportion of perhaps ten to one, and conscription into the "American People's Army" will have drained millions of able-bodied young men from the normal work force. Farms will have been particularly effected, with the result that unskilled manual labor on the land, as elsewhere, will rely to a great extent on women.

Filmmaker

Conditions with regard to schooling, registration in a union, and State control, are the same as those for painters and sculptors (see *Artist*). Film style will be that of socialist realism. Directors who attempt to be too clever and are caught by the censor or secret police will suffer the same penalty as given such men as Sergei Paradjanov, maker of two of the few interesting modern Soviet films, *Sayat Nova* and *Shadows of Our Forgotten Ancestors*. In January 1974, he was arrested and sent to a labor camp on a charge of homosexuality. It is KGB policy, when destroying a person on political or other grounds, to discredit them morally for good measure. (See also *Actor, Musician.*)

Financier or Financial Consultant (see *Banker; Businessperson*)

Fireman

State employee. Lower salary. No strikes.

Funeral Director

Services will be speedy, drab, and uniform. Atheist forms of committal will be encouraged, religious forms banned or perfunctorily performed. Mortuary "chapels" will be secularized, and only in rare cases will services be carried out in cathedrals, churches, chapels, or other religious buildings, the majority of which will in any case be closed or devoted to nonreligious uses (see *Clergy*). However, Communist burials, while lacking frills, will at least be inexpensive.

You will eventually become a state employee.

Furniture Maker or Dealer

The majority of furniture stores will close. Most citizens will lack the funds to buy new furniture and will make do with what they have. The furniture industry will be State-owned, and when it gets back on its feet, its products will be of poor quality and indifferent design.

Garage or Gas Station Owner or Employee

As we saw in the last chapter, private motoring will have enormously decreased. There will be very few cars on the roads and consequently no need for a large number of gas stations. The oil companies will in any case be nationalized, and there will be only one brand and probably only one grade of gas. Even large cities will possess only a handful of gas stations, usually tucked away in obscure and inconvenient spots. (The elite will have their own gas stations, limousines, and chauffeurs.) Although there are fewer cars, production and servicing standards will be

107

such that motor mechanics' skills will be saleable on the black market. And you may also try your hand at, and profit by, the repairing and refurbishing of bicycles.

Hawaiian

Because of the strategic importance of Hawaii, halfway between the United States and China and in a position to dominate the Pacific, stringent measures will be called for. The able-bodied members of the population, including the native Hawaiians, will join a "voluntary" defense organization to build, in their spare time, underground bunkers and fortifications or to enlarge and strengthen those that already exist. The remainder are likely to be shipped to the mainland as with Japanese-Americans (see below). In time, Hawaii will most probably be seeded with Russian colonists in order to make it totally secure. Old Russian claims to the islands are likely to be revised, and direct annexation to the USSR is probable, as will also be the case with Alaska. (The USSR has annexed territory from all the Communist countries on which it borders.)

Homosexual

Male homosexuality is illegal under all Communist regimes. The usual sentence will be five to ten years in a labor camp. As with other regulations, this will not be invariably enforced if political considerations make it convenient in individual cases to proceed otherwise. The regime occasionally prefers to secure the collaboration of the homosexual by holding the other alternative over him. In the takeover period, the police will probably be too busy to pay much attention to the persecution of homosexuals in general, but gay liberation and organizations designed to promote their interests will at once be banned, and those who attempt to persist with them will be instantly arrested.

Hospital Employee (see Dentist; Doctor)

Hotel Owner or Employee

Hotel owners will be dispossessed and, if they are fortunate, may be given employment in lower grades of the industry. Those hotels that are permitted to continue will operate in a notably run-down condition, although some of the luxury hotels will be maintained at a level somewhat below their best in order to cater to the Soviet and Communist elite and other important visitors. In these major establishments, all rooms will be bugged, with a special central office listening in at all times. Only "cleared" and reliable staff will remain, and they will be required to act as government informers. In ordinary hotels, also State-run, jobs will be available at a reduced salary, but there will be less work to perform as little service will be given beyond the provision of a more-or-less clean room.

Indian (Native American)

The Communists will make what use they can of Indians and the Indian movements, although they will not have the priority given to the more numerous black and Chicano elements.

The reservations, probably renamed "autonomous areas," will be maintained, but the inhabitants will have no right to the oil and other resources in them, which will be the property of the

State. And there will no longer be any bar to white or other settlers. The Indians will become citizens, although of course, the advantages of citizenship will be few. A few select Indians will be given impressive-looking posts, largely of a cosmetic nature; for example, there will be an Indian commissioner for native American affairs together with a number of Congressmen of the new style.

Indian organizations will be purged of any independent elements of leadership. As the record of the tribes and many subgroups in the Soviet Union shows, it will be difficult to find any Indians who are real Communists, or even near-Communists, to be heads of the administration of the autonomous areas; the Communists will have to make do with supervision by unobtrusive white "advisers." Indian languages, dances, customs, and folkways will be encouraged but guided into the desired channels. For example, new "folk songs" will be required, extolling the virtues of communism. At the same time, as elsewhere, Indians will be forced into collective farms. Those who live a mobile existence, such as the Navajo, will be compelled to settle.

In general, the interests of the State economy will be put before those of the small peoples. A Soviet commentator has written of similar groups in areas in the mountains bordering China:

> The present-day Khakassi living in the Khakass Autonomous Province are a minority in the national composition of Khakassia. The non-Khakassian population in Khakassia forms a majority and outnumbers the Khakassi several times. This has occurred during the last twenty years chiefly because the Khakassi, few in number, were not in a position to ensure the rapid development of a powerful industry having All-Union and All-State importance, for the establishment of which favourable local conditions exist. This is also applicable to the Shors . . . and the Altais of the High Altai Autonomous Province . . . It is

difficult to say what will be the ultimate fate of each of the small ethnographic groups and peoples . . .

But not too difficult to guess; and for Khakass, Shor, Altai, read, in the American context, Navajo, Hopi, Apache.

In the Soviet Union, mountain and desert peoples like the Chechens and Kalmyks, resembling many of the Western Indians, were driven into a more desperate resistance than that of any section of the population; and several were among those later deported en masse (men, women and children) to Siberia, although some of these were later allowed to return.

Meanwhile, those of you who inhabit mountain or desert country will possess certain advantages in that it will be difficult to keep you under constant observation and control. Our advice is: Keep your more unassimilable customs and folkways as far out of sight as possible; take what you are given; do not be deceived by temporary advantages; and unless you are desperate, do not offer resistance. But you will be prepared, if you do become desperate, to revert to the guerrilla-type existence of your forefathers. You should be more successful than most.

Industrial Worker

In theory, you will be the bulwark of the new socialist America.

You and everyone else will read a vast amount of propaganda about your heroic efforts in industry, and about your devoted loyalty to the new "workers' state." Control of your organizations will be the major concern of the Communist party (see *Trade Unionist*).

All this will have some slight advantages, up to a point. Over minor offenses, for example, you will be treated comparatively lightly. With major matters such as opposition to the regime, on the other hand, your status will count against you since you will have proved yourself a "traitor to your class." After the needs and wishes of the new bureaucratic elite have been satisfied, your children will, in the first decade or so have preferential access to education and indoctrination.

You will find a good many changes in your work. Trade unions will be totally under Communist control, and while they will administer holiday and insurance funds, they will have no right to oppose the management. The basic rule to which everything else must cede is the fulfillment of the "plan." Since this is allotted from Washington, it will often be unrealistic, and you will be forced to work a great deal of overtime, almost invariably without special payment—especially toward the end of each month.

You will be issued a "labor book" that will list your successive jobs, with each management's comments on your reasons for being transferred, including censure.

It has been the industrial working class above all, in spite of the pretenses of the Communist party, which has been the backbone of resistance in the Communist lands; as in Plzeň and East Berlin in 1953, in Budapest and Poznan in 1956, in Gdansk and elsewhere in 1970, and finally in the great Polish Solidarity movement today—to name some major worker militancy in Soviet-controlled countries. And in the Soviet Union itself, huge worker outbreaks have taken place in the last couple of decades in places like Novocherkassk, Temir-Tau, Krivoy Rog, Dneprodzerzhinsk.

These are signs that the worker does not really do very well out of the system administered in his name. But they also show that in certain circumstances worker unrest can spearhead major revolt against the regime. It is notable that some of the most powerful outbursts, even in the USSR itself, have come when economic resentment has been linked with political resentment—some Soviet riots and strikes were touched off by economic suffering, others by workers' resentment at their colleagues being jailed and beaten to death by the police. But the most powerful movements of all have taken place when worker resentment has been linked with national hatred of the Soviet occupier. You will probably find this to be the case in America.

Insurance Agent or Insurance Company Employee

Insurance companies will be immediately nationalized and their capital confiscated. Insurance will become a prerogative of the State or its subsidiary, the "Trade Unions," and you may be employed in the State insurance organization.

Japanese American

If Japan has not been conquered, all Japanese Americans will be regarded as adherents of a hostile power. They will automatically be deported from the Hawaiian Islands, California, and the other Pacific states. This will remind the older among them of their fates in 1942, with the difference that similar deportations under Soviet rule have resulted in an average 30 percent death rate.

Jewish

Many Jewish groups will find themselves in immediate trouble for a wide variety of reasons. They may be capitalists or involved in non-Communist politics or, in the specifically Jewish context, be Zionists or rabbis. Even if you have not given offense in any of these respects, you will inevitably find yourself, if you are

Jewish, in a paradoxical situation. As with every other "ethnic" group, there will be an effort to use your organizations over the transitional stage; yet, at the same time, you will automatically be more suspect than your Gentile equivalent. This even applies to the Jewish Communist, who will be regarded with more distrust than his Gentile comrade when it comes to sniffing out deviation. So, unless you are an exceptional creature who can be manipulated as a "show Jew" and as a docile "leader" of the Jewish community, your prospects are shaky. This is not to say that every Jew will be arrested (though such a plan does seem to have existed in the Soviet Union in 1953), or even that you will automatically lose your job; but it does mean that certain professions will be largely or wholly closed to you. The maintenance of your Jewish identity will be discouraged, the Hebrew language will be virtually banned, and while Yiddish will be permitted, no Yiddish theatres will be open and no Yiddish books will be printed, although a few small-circulation Yiddish Communist newspapers will probably survive. As for anti-Semites, they will, of course, provided they can pass muster on other grounds, be very welcome to the regime, particularly as propagandists.

John Birch Society Member

Your life will, of course, be automatically forfeit. However, if you are determined to preserve it at all costs, your chances are a good deal better than those of, say, the Maoists or the Trotskyites (see below) at the other end of the political spectrum. In East Germany, large numbers of ex-Nazis were admitted to the Communist party, to some extent because the Nazis and the Communists had similar authoritarian affinities but, more importantly, because, to save themselves, the Nazis had nowhere else to go; and the Communists were glad to accept them since they needed any recruits they could get. (At one time the Communist Central Committee, the highest organ of the DDR, contained fourteen ex-Nazis to merely two ex-Social Democrats.) Even more encouraging is the example of Piasecki, once the leader of the very small and very extreme Polish Fascist party. When he fell into Russian hands, he was told by Ivan Serov himself, deputy head of the Soviet secret police, that he was as good as dead already, but if he agreed to collaborate, the Russians could use him. He was made head of PAX, a body directed toward the subversion of the Catholic Church and, at the same time, was allowed or encouraged to carry out private financial transactions that made him the richest man in Poland. So you can see that there is no need to despair, and that, paradoxically, if you are a right-wing politician with a strong anti-Communist record, you may yet have a better future (at least for the time being) than many of your more "progressive" colleagues. As in the case of Piasecki, you can take additional heart from the case of Tatarescu in Romania. He had actually been a signatory of Hitler's Anti-Comintern Pact; but while Socialists and moderates were being arrested, the Russians made him foreign minister, a post that he managed to hold for some years.

Journalist (Newspaper, Magazine, TV)

If you are a political columnist or commentator, or have otherwise become known for ideas antipathetic to the Communist view, you will have little chance of remaining at liberty. Anyhow, you will have no future in journalism. If the offense you have committed is judged to be minor, you might be able to secure some sort of job in the bureaucracy. We would suggest that you acquire some appropriate skill such as bookkeeping.

If your field has been reasonably far removed from politics, however, you may be allowed to carry on for a time until you can be replaced by a young Communist who has been trained to present your subject in an impeccable Marxist-Leninist light.

Censorship will be imposed immediately on the arrival of the Russians and all "anti-Soviet" staff will be turned off. Newspapers that are considered to have had a particularly anti-Soviet bias will be expropriated and handed over to the Communist party or some other Communist-sponsored organization. In any case, one or other of the main newspapers and television stations in each locality will be delivered up to the Party and renamed. Those non-Communist papers and stations allowed to survive will be given the task of representing the views of the "Democratic" and "Republican" parties which form part of the "coalition" government until they too fade away.

Ku Klux Klan Member

Your organization will be suppressed. Trials will be held in Washington and in the South in which men totally without KKK sympathy or background will be branded as such. The Soviet authorities will have little use for real KKK members, who are seldom as "literate" as John Birchers (see above); but those who have specialized in anti-Semitism and have any journalistic or demagogic flair may come to some arrangement, and be retrospectively proved not to have been KKK men at all.

Lawyer

Lawyers will, in general, be regarded as a hostile class element. This will be more so in their case than similar strata because so many of them are involved in the public life of pre-Occupation America and concerned with rights, balances, constitutionality, and common law—all totally opposed to the Communist principle.

Casualties, therefore, will be high.

However, under the leadership of lawyers already of Communist persuasion, of whom there are some, a new body of lawyers will be built up, in which, if you survive and are able to accept education in the newer legal principles, you may obtain employment.

Some lawyers will be needed, especially those with the histrionic talents of an Andrei Vishinsky, for the upcoming series of spectacular show trials. Compliant judges will also be required.

The profession will, naturally, be brought under control like the others. A well-purged "bar association" will be headed by Communist officials. Judges at all levels who are still at their posts after the first phase will be replaced "constitutionally." Where they are at present elected, Communist-style elections will provide suitable replacements. Where they are appointed, as with the Supreme Court and so forth, the new political leaders will act accordingly.

The new judges will interpret the Constitution to suit the wishes of the occupying power and the processes of Sovietization.

Should any constitutional amendments be required, they will be dealt with by the puppet Congress and through fake popular votes. In fact, Communist-type constitutions are full of the same sort of guarantees of civic rights as are to be found in the present Constitution of the United States. But a few changes will nevertheless be necessary—in particular, say, a Thirtieth and Thirty-first Amendment, respectively—institutionalizing the Soviet economic system and officially making the Communist party the central power in the land.

If you do continue to practice, you will have to change your courtroom style. In a Soviet-type court, especially where there is any trace whatever of a political tinge to the case, lawyers are not

117

expected to get into arguments. The defense lawyer, in particular, is supposed to represent not so much the interests of his client as those of the community; and there have been many cases under this system in which they have strongly dissociated themselves from their client's pleas of innocence.

You will not, moreover, be operating in a private and independent capacity. You will be a member of the "collegium" of lawyers in your area, paid and controlled by the State, and allotted to clients as suits the authorities.

Unless you have a very strong stomach, therefore, our advice would be that you abandon the profession at the outset. So you should now put your mind to training yourself for some other means of supporting your family.

Librarian

Your job will be comparatively safe, if you can bear the conditions imposed on you. Your first duty will be to carry out the removal from your shelves of a large part of their contents. Politically unsuitable books, together with those considered pornographic or decadent, will be proscribed; you will be surprised at the manner in which the labels of pornography and decadence have been extended to cover a very wide range of literature. Your old reference books, such as encyclopedias, will be withdrawn and pulped.

You should keep handy a pair of sharp scissors and a supply of paste as you will have to cut out or replace those entries in the new style encyclopedias and reference books that become politically inconvenient—a normal Soviet practice. As the years go by, even the more harmless books on your shelves will be gradually replaced as works commissioned and printed by the State begin to appear in adequate numbers. Experience from the Soviet Union and particularly from Eastern European countries sug-

118

gests that you will not be kept very busy checking these out. If you can safely save and secrete some of the books that are being discarded, well and good; although your superiors will be on the lookout for this, and it may be hazardous for you or your friends to be caught reading them.

Duplicating machines will be usable by designated staff only, and will be available, even to this degree, only in major libraries.

Maoist

Prospects minimal. Emigrate or die.

Military

Like the *Lawyer* (above), as a member of one of the principal mainstays and upholders of the American way of life you will be in an unenviable position. Every officer above and including the rank of colonel or naval commander will be detained and will face the probability of being shot. It would therefore be wise to take any early opportunity to seek refuge in a free or neutral country, if any exists and you can get to it. Naval officers should attempt to sail their ships to safe ports, and air force pilots should attempt to head their planes for unoccupied territory.

If this is impossible, as soon after the debacle as you can, you should divest yourself of your uniform and bury it or otherwise get rid of it. You will not want to figure in an American equivalent of the Katyn massacres, in which, in peacetime, fifteen thousand Polish officers had their wrists bound behind their backs with barbed wire and were shot in open ditches. You might also hide or bury whatever arms you possess in a marked spot, in the rather unlikely event that you ever get a chance to return one day and dig them up. Beg, borrow, or steal a suit of civilian clothes;

119

then try to fade unobtrusively into the background, losing yourself in the turmoil around you.

It would be a good idea to try to prepare beforehand a false name, a cover story, and perhaps a false set of papers. In the end you may well be tracked down by the KGB, unless you can escape abroad; but when this happens, enough time may have elapsed for some kind of modified amnesty to have come about, under which you will be eligible only for a term in a labor camp rather than outright execution.

After the American surrender, all the lower ranks, noncommissioned as well as commissioned, will be processed for longer or shorter periods in reeducation camps, where they will be subjected to intensive rectification of their former capitalist illusions. If you appear to be compliant, act slightly stupid, and your recantation and ideological progress are considered satisfactory, you will either be given your discharge papers or inducted into the American People's Army.

This will have been formed from the rump of the old United States forces, with American, or near-American commanders— some of them without military experience. New draftees will get only three or four dollars a week, if that, but at least in a time of uncertainty they will have a roof over their heads, sound clothes, and a far better ration of food than the civilian population.

Apart from the strategic (missile) forces, which will be taken over intact by the Soviet authorities with all American cadres dismissed at once, the new American People's Army will include all arms. It will go through a period of intensive purging and equally intensive training under fraternal Soviet instructors. Gradually, as increasing numbers of Communists and Communist sympathizers receive military training, it will be expanded until it can become a useful auxiliary to the Soviet army. In a few years, as in other Soviet colonies, it will be possible to enlarge the new intake until the United States forces (still so called) will be available for Soviet purposes abroad. They will never be regarded as wholly reliable, and secret police security will be extremely thorough, but will nevertheless—and even more for that reason—be thrown into situations where cannon fodder, literally, will be the immediate requirement. In addition to being "advised" by the Russians, you may also find yourself being "advised" by the East Germans since the latter, with their blind discipline, goose-stepping, and general Nazi antecedents have in recent years emerged as the drillmasters of satellite Communist armies, whether in Europe or Africa. Thus Americans, as with von Steuben and his staff in the American Revolution, may once again find themselves obeying Prussian mentors, although hardly in the cause of freedom. You may also be, out of necessity, taking orders from Cubans.

You will serve wherever the Soviet cause dictates.

Conscientious objection will be illegal.

Musician

Music does not speak such a direct and potentially subversive language as literature, so it will not be visited with the same degree of severity. Nevertheless all composers and executive musicians will be supervised through their respective "unions." If you are a composer and want to be performed, you should forget serial, atonal, aleatory, or other modern techniques. You will find it particularly exasperating to be bullied by fifth-rate composers who occupy positions of power in your union, as occurred with Tikhon Khrennikov, then as now first secretary of the Soviet Composers' Union, who was encouraged by the oafish Zhdanov to torment musicians of the caliber of Prokofiev and Shostakovich, whom he berated as if they were small boys. As a reward, his tawdry music is regularly performed behind the Iron Curtain, where captive audiences are bidden to applaud it as if it was Beethoven. Even so, classical composers and musicians will be in a better position than popular ones. Much popular music will be banned as "decadent," and such phenomena as rock concerts will naturally not be licensed. On the other hand, a new type of folk music will emerge, complete with pro-Soviet words and sentiments.

Native American (see Indian)

Navy (see Military)

New Left

You will confront the Russians with a problem slightly different from any that they have previously had to cope with. Generally speaking, yours will be treated in the same way as the more orthodox Socialist bodies, though to the extent that you hold principles advocating a type of socialism radically different from and ideologically competitive with that of the Communists, you will be among the first to face arrest. Otherwise, your organizations, such as they are, will be merged first with those of a new pro-Communist "Socialist party" and then with the Communist party itself.

In any case, you should meanwhile, we feel, make some attempt to come to terms with reality. For example, the Communist party line will not embrace pot smoking, homosexuality, hardly even beards. Therefore, if you are an adherent of the New Left, you should consider (1) getting rid of your drugs, (2) concealing your deviant proclivities, and (3) shaving off your whiskers.

Optometrist (see and compare Dentist)

122

Pet Shop Operator

It is unlikely that families will be able to spare any scraps of food for feeding pets, let alone extra money for grooming them or purchasing accessories. The various pet industries will be closed down, and most cats and dogs will have to be put to sleep or allowed to run free and take their chances. After the fighting ends, there will, in any case, be a serious infestation of ownerless dogs running in wild packs with which the authorities will have to deal. Owners of pet shops should lose no time making plans for alternative employment.

Pharmacist (see and compare *Dentist; Doctor*)

Photographer

Supplies will be scarce and unrestricted photographing will, in any case, be severely discouraged. The professional photographers still permitted to operate will be licensed by the State and their output closely scrutinized and controlled.

But there will be considerable demand for photographs of important persons and ceremonies of the new order, and press photography will flourish. You must, however, be ready to abandon "frank" photographs showing politicians from unflattering angles or in awkward or silly movements.

For the photographer not directly employed on a paper, there will also be outlets. The new elite always show an endless appetite for professional-style visual representation of themselves and various aspects of their power and position. You may also find that ordinary families will seek, more than usual, records of their loved ones, in the constant fear that they may be separated at any time by death or deportation. (In labor camps it

123

has often been possible for prisoners to keep small photographs, which have given them some cheer and comfort.)

If you are skilled at montage and general faking of photographs, you may be employed as a specialist on one of the main newspapers or agencies. It is traditional in Communist countries to issue historical and other photographs with changes made to eliminate faces of those who have meanwhile fallen into disfavor or to enhance the status of those who have risen. Cases in the USSR, going back fifty years but practiced to this day, include the mere omission, by brushing out, of major leaders of the revolution like Trotsky; the substitution of a tree for a famous former comrade, Lev Kamenev, in a reproduction of a famous prerevolution photograph; the moving of Georgi Malenkov, a comparatively minor figure when the photo was first printed, to standing alone with Stalin and Mao Tse-tung through the removal of half a dozen intervening figures when Malenkov had become prime minister; the insertion of a nonexistent beard on a figure of unclear status, F. Khodzhayev, in the edited version of a group picture; and quite recently, the transformation of one of a group of five astronauts into a doorpost. So if you have talents in this direction, you may have a prosperous career.

Poison Pen

You will have splendid opportunities to ruin your neighbors, colleagues, and friends by writing anonymous denunciations which have always been much valued in Communist circles, to the secret police. The facts you retail need not in any way be truthful, but it will be nonetheless advantageous to be able to include genuine remarks made by your victims in which they express dissatisfaction with some aspect of the Occupation. If you want to cause even more harm, you can offer your services to the secret police as a "Seksot" or a regular paid informer and collaborator. (Well-organized networks of these "Seksoti" will be set up, covering every area of the United States.)

Policeman

All senior officers will be replaced, and there will be arrests and executions of those of whatever rank who had previously been engaged in combating subversion, putting down riots, or otherwise engaging in "political" activities in support of the previous government. Soviet sympathizers will be given all major posts, and police everywhere will come under the centralized control of a new Department of the Interior in Washington. Some cadres of the regular detective force will be retained, under Soviet direction, until they can be replaced by Communist collaborators. Many traffic police and highway patrols will be laid off since there will be few cars or trucks on the road except those of the occupier, which will move largely in a convoy.

The police will be concerned with issuing permits required for internal travel and with checking on those from out of town registering at hotels and will take on a large staff for such purposes.

The border patrol, together with the immigration service, will come under the direct jurisdiction of the secret police in Washington, who may keep on reliable Americans and seek to recruit more. Movement across national borders will be extremely restricted—unless, in the case of Canada, it is thought convenient to "unite" it with the United States. The Mexican border, in any event, will be equipped with a formidable barbed-wire fence, with watchtowers and searchlights at frequent intervals.

In the course of time, a new special police force of considerable size will be equipped with modern weapons, up to and including light tanks and artillery. This force will be used as the first line in putting down demonstrations or risings against the Occupation, with the Red Army held in reserve.

Priest (see Clergyman)

Printer

Your skills will be much in demand by the authorities. There will be an enormous increase in the number of forms, permits, and general bureaucratic papers. Even more, there will be an enormous output of propaganda material of every type: pamphlets, posters, leaflets, booklets, and books by the hundreds of millions. The main newspapers will appear in enormous editions, again in several millions, even when they are virtually unreadable. Though real circulation will go down, there will be a large forced circulation to all Party and official bodies and individuals, while in the absence of other information, some citizens will continue to buy the papers.

All printing machines and all printing matter will be under very strict control. Unofficial possession of even the smallest press or duplicating machine will be illegal.

Psychiatrist

Western psychiatry is ill regarded in the Soviet Union, and most psychiatry in the present sense will cease and the files of its practitioners will be turned over to the secret police as possible sources of evidence. A Soviet-style psychiatry will take its place, and for those Western psychiatrists who contrive to adapt their theories to Soviet ideology, a small clientele of rich Party officials and their families will be a source of fees. But the massive employment of psychiatry will cease, and you are advised to think about developing other skills. On the other hand, an ambitious and unscrupulous psychiatrist might do well by gaining employment in one of the special police psychiatric hospitals where certain offenders are held and subjected to psychochemical abuse (see chapter 3).

Psychopath

If you are able and prepared to control yourself in all matters where you might offend the authorities, a wide field of activity of a type you will find rewarding will remain open to you. Those not afflicted with consciences will be much in demand not only in occupations offering opportunities of violence (see *Sadist*) but also in all other institutions, where it will always be possible to denounce anyone who stands in the way of your desires or to blackmail them into submitting.

Indeed, the Soviet system as consolidated by Stalin and perpetuated by his successors has been described as a psychopathocracy. If your condition is of the right type, you might rise very high indeed in the new hierarchy.

Publisher

There will be a short interim period before all publishing firms are brought under control of one or another of the Communist-sponsored organizations. But there will be an immediate ban on all "anti-Soviet" literature. Publishers will find that this is interpreted to cover any independent work whatever in the fields of history, economics, politics, and social thought—just as almost all modern American fiction will be banned as "pornographic."

Many publishers will in any case have been arrested for their earlier purveying of books warning America of the Soviet threat or simply retailing facts about the Soviet regime. Those firms that survive will be taken over as soon as practicable. The new Communist-controlled "writers' union" will own directly, or through local branches, most of the firms printing literary works proper. The publishing of political, military works, and so forth will come under direct government control; political works being published by the State political publishers, military works by the Department of Defense, and so forth.

If you continue to work in these institutions, you will have to be careful not to offend the censorship. Sticking to the general guidelines will not be sufficient, and even these new Communist-controlled organizations will not be trusted in this sensitive area.

There will be a large body of censors—in Russia it is estimated that there are about seventy thousand of these. Every printed word must be examined by a representative of the Board of Censorship and certified correct before publication. In the case of a book there is first a "precensorship." If it passes this, some twenty copies may then be printed, after which the presses will be locked and copies sent for approval to a variety of governmental agencies and departments of the Communist party, always including the secret police. When and if all these have approved, printing may take place.

The censors will be guided by an instruction book (the Polish one consists of 700 pages) listing the things that may not be mentioned. These will naturally include anything discreditable about the Soviet Union, the Communist party, and so forth— and in particular any atrocity committed by the Soviet army, any information about the now-flourishing labor camps, any hints that everybody is not happy under the Occupation. There will also be a number of named persons to whom one may not refer because for one reason or another they are in disfavor.

Puerto Rican

Puerto Ricans will, to some degree, be a special case since Puerto Rico itself will probably become an "autonomous" republic in a Caribbean federation dominated by Soviet Cuba. The important Puerto Rican communities in New York and elsewhere will be tightly organized under Communist control, and Puerto Rican Communists will be given a fair proportion of local administrative posts, as with blacks. (See also *Chicano, etc.*)

Rabbi

Your position will be, as we have suggested, among the worst in religious categories. You should, more than most others, pay particular attention to our advice in preparing for prison and labor camp. (See also *Clergymen; Jew.*)

Radio Station Operator or Employee (see Television)

Realtor

Private ownership of property and land will be abolished and a decree of total nationalization will immediately go into force. Real estate dealing will thereupon become inoperative.

Restaurant Owner or Worker

A few top-class restaurants will remain in business and, even in famine times, will be provided, for the edification of the Soviet and Communist elite, with a plentiful supply of provisions, including luxuries. Otherwise restaurants and eateries in general may continue under private ownership for a year or so until full nationalization and Sovietization has taken place. However, keeping them supplied will entail your being in constant attendance at the local rationing offices and the necessity for continuous bribes and payoffs.

The prices you will have to charge will probably be beyond the pockets of most citizens, although there will always be a quota of minor officials, police, and so on who will prefer to eat anything and to eat anywhere in preference to their own dreary canteens.

Many cooks and waiters will find that they have no choice left but to work in such canteens, where conditions are notoriously poor, hours indeterminate, and pay minimal. However, wretched though working in State canteens may be, it possesses one advantage not to be despised: access to food. Employees will always be suspected of stealing, and suspected correctly, but the Soviet habit is not to try to enforce the unenforceable in such spheres unless they have some other reason for getting rid of somebody—or unless instructions for a strict purge have come down and they are looking for easily compromised victims.

Eventually the whole restaurant network will be run by the Department of Internal Trade, and quality will suffer accordingly, though restaurateurs who manage to work in them will, as we say, at least eat.

Russian American

Though some will be used by the occupiers as interpreters, and even in political posts, Americans of Russian descent can look forward to especially virulent treatment. We will draw a veil over what will happen to former Russian defectors who fall into Soviet hands.

Sadist

Although the secret police will have some use for torturers, such positions are unlikely to be open except to men with political acumen and training, but low-grade thugs, known as "boxers," are often employed for routine beatings. Guards will be needed, of course, on a large scale for the new labor camp and prison system and will be more or less free to maltreat prisoners at their leisure. You should be warned, on the other hand, that most of the labor camps are likely to be situated in the most distant and forbidding parts of the continent.

If you apply for a post as an executioner, you might be enrolled in one of the municipal firing squads. Your opportunity to carry out individual executions, if such is your taste, will probably be somewhat restricted. The traditional Soviet method of executing single offenders is by means of a bullet in the back of the neck and is invariably conducted neatly and expeditiously by a specialist of officer rank. Mass executions are bound, of course, to occur, and you may well be given a chance to participate in some of them.

Schoolteacher

Under *Academic* we have dealt with the situation of the university teacher. In preuniversity education, teachers will find that things are, generally speaking, similar.

Instruction in mathematics will continue much as before, but

131

most other subjects will have new textbooks and new curricula. Many texts in English literature will be withdrawn, and there will be an emphasis on Soviet and Communist authors of the social realist persuasion, most of whose works will have the texture of sawdust.

You too will have to teach your pupils versions of history that are entirely untrue. You too will have to lead them in ceremonies of loyalty to the regime. You will spend hours on teachers' committees in which ways of improving the political education of the children is discussed. But, except in the highest classes, you will not have to teach "Marxism-Leninism" as such, merely a set of easily assimilated ideas, a sort of Communist pap or pabulum. You will find that the Party administrators in charge of you are a low-grade lot since the more educated ones will be spread thin in the universities and elsewhere. They will intervene in the clumsiest and most irritating manner. You must not retort in kind.

Be careful of the temptation, while teaching nonsense, to make your true view of it clear to your students by your tone of voice or the expression on your face. One Soviet instruction typical of many, runs:

> One must not content oneself with merely paying attention to *what* is being said, for that may well be in complete harmony with the Party program. One must pay attention also to the *manner*—to the sincerity, for example, with which a schoolmistress recites a poem the authorities regard as doubtful, or the pleasure revealed by a critic who goes into detail about a play he professes to condemn.

Your position will bring you some particularly difficult problems. First, children are more easily influenced than older people, and you will find at least a few of your pupils beginning to believe what they are told day in and day out. You will be

132

tempted to guide them unobtrusively toward the truth. If you do, be sure to be very careful indeed. Once children are persuaded that it is their duty to report you for deviation, it takes little to persuade them to denounce you. There are always smug, nasty-minded children with grudges against everybody, but especially teachers.

Second, you will also find the opposite problem: many children, especially the younger ones, may blurt out true facts or express their true feelings. You will wish to do all you can to protect them and to protect their families from whom they probably imbibed these "errors." Yet you will have to tell them that they are wrong while making every excuse for them.

This will all be a very harrowing experience, and it is no wonder that teachers have been among the most severely purged professions in all Communist countries. After a while, if you keep your job, you will adjust as best you can. And you will find as time goes by that the children too have adjusted to the situation and no longer betray themselves. As for the minority whom you regretfully see passing from your hands as offensively loyal robots of the regime, do not worry too much. Some, indeed, will go on to become the new generation of Soviet auxiliaries. But many, even those who may be at their worst at sixteen, will become disillusioned as students or in early adulthood.

Military and civil-defense training will be compulsory in all schools, and you will be required to help where necessary.

Scientist

Certain sciences, such as astronomy, will be comparatively free from official intrusion, but most will be subject to State intervention. If you are a practicing scientist in any field particularly useful to the Soviet Union, you are likely to be deported there, although you will be handled more or less with kid gloves as you

133

will be regarded in the same light as valuable livestock. Once in the Soviet Union, you will be housed in comfortable circumstances in special isolated communities, in the Urals or in Siberia. Provided you behave yourself and work hard, you will be well treated as long as your line of research proves fruitful.

Whether you work for the Russians in the USSR or the United States, you will encounter continuous trouble among your Party managers at all levels. Avoid getting involved in all such backbiting and squabbling and devote yourself, as far as possible, to your own concerns. You are, after all, purely as a scientist, likely to find your work absorbing, and it will help you to forget your troubles. You will find it disturbing and infuriating to be herded into mass projects, harangued by officials, and given timetables and deadlines; but as long as you toe the line, you will probably be able to continue with your own line of research, whatever it is, at least for part of the time, and you may be able to overlook the fact that whatever advances you help to bring about will be put to use to increase still further the powers of a tyrannical regime.

The sting may also be lessened by the sympathy of your Soviet colleagues, most of whom will be sensitive people who silently regard themselves as being in the same boat. Now that Soviet science has come of age, there is less likelihood than formerly that you will become trapped in one of the crasser controversies. Vavilov, the great biologist, fell foul of the quack Lysenko, whose theories were endorsed by Stalin, and he died in the Gulag. Stalin also espoused the peculiar theories of the linguist Marr, who claimed that all language derived from only four basic sounds, and many scholars fell foul of the dictator in consequence and wound up in jail. In modern circumstances, the probability of such bizarre episodes has lessened, but the Central Committee still has the last word in scientific matters. You should be alert and try not to get yourself entangled in controversy. Many scientists, mathematicians, and so on are now in jail or exile in the USSR for applying their reasoning powers to political and social matters. Do not despise the minor skills you may have picked up, such as the ability to repair electrical equipment. If you are purged, this may be valuable even in a labor camp, while elsewhere it may provide you with an income.

Socialist

Socialists with ideas about socialism different from the definition of that form of society thought correct by the Soviet authorities will suffer earlier and more severely than mere democrats and capitalists. The leaders of the Eastern European Socialists are mostly dead or in prison, and all their parties have long since been extinguished.

But at first, for a time, the Russians will encourage a Socialist party. It will have as its leadership, if possible, a few prominent members of the present movement with the addition of a few secret Communists. All the smaller Socialist sects will probably be incorporated into it, as we said in an earlier chapter, at a conference run on "constitutional" lines. Those attending the conference will be rendered amenable both by simple, direct pressure and by the absence due to the arrest of those Socialists who have previously shown themselves strongly opposed to the Soviet system.

Within two to three years, any remaining Socialist leaders inclined to show any sign of independence will be eliminated, and the Socialists will be merged (once again "voluntarily") with the Communist party. A very few Socialist leaders will be accorded positions in the new organization. These, of course, will be men who have already collaborated unreservedly. Even so, few of them will last long. Some will vanish into oblivion, others into the labor camps and prisons, as did the stooge Arpad Szakasits, who betrayed the Hungarian Social Democratic party to the Communists.

135

Student

You will not get to college if your parents have been classified as social or political undesirables. Children of working-class parents will in principle enjoy preference over middle-class parents, but in fact, the children of collaborators and Party functionaries will have priority, whatever their scholastic abilities. (And the employment by the Communist rich of teachers wishing to supplement their salaries by private tutoring will give them a certain advantage even there.) For ordinary students, as against the children of Party members, the entrance requirements will be stricter than they are now. The curriculum will be drab and examinations will be strenuous. Punctual and regular attendance in class will be obligatory, especially in the courses in Marxism-Leninism. Military and paramilitary training will take place, although this will be in addition to, not in place of, the normal two years of military service that will precede or follow the years at the university. Students will be expected to be polite, and their clothes and personal grooming will be in accord with the institutional dress code. The student leadership will be appointed by the Communist administration, and student protests, strikes, sit-ins, and other demonstrations will be promptly and unequivocally put down if they occur. Offenders will be dismissed from college and sent to jail. Students will also be liable to free and "voluntary" service to the State; for example, at the times of planting and harvesting you can be sent to work for ten hours a day and for a month or six weeks at a time, in the fields with the regular farm workers, picking potatoes, cabbages, beets, and other row crops. This will keep you physically fit but will interfere somewhat with your studies.

As the system settles down, a flourishing market in examination papers, professional examination sitters, and so on will arise. If, even so, you fail your examinations, it will often be possible to buy fake credentials. Influential parents will usually be able to obtain improved marks for their children through threats or bribes—a perennial scandal in the USSR today. (See also *Youth.*)

Surgeon (see Doctor)

Technician (see Engineer)

Television Station Owner or Employee (see Journalist)

Trade Unionist (see Industrial Worker)

Honest trade union leaders will be bustled off at once to the labor camps. Crooked ones, who can be expected to be familiar with the strong-arm tactics called for in the first days of the Occupation, will last longer. The smaller craft unions will be abolished and those that remain will be concentrated into large, streamlined corporations with all leading posts under direct Party and secret police control. Trade union conferences will rapidly become spectacles at which the decrees and policies of the Party will be ecstatically and unanimously rubber-stamped. This in fact will be the chief function of the trade unions: to facilitate the control, discipline, and unity of the workforce. Questions of pay and working conditions will be of secondary importance and will in practice be the concern of Party officials. To resist or question the decisions of the employer, who will now be the State, will bring you penalties.

The leaders of the Soviet Union are peculiarly sensitive, as the leaders of Communist America will be, to defiance by the workers since it represents the most alarming of the challenges that might be made to their supremacy and right to govern. According to Marxist-Leninist theory, such defiance should simply not occur, so it is very disturbing when it does, and the authorities will react sharply. You should take this into account before you decide to embark on strikes, slowdowns, pay disputes, and all similar overt forms of industrial action, let alone form any genuine union. Remember too that informers and agents provocateurs will be everywhere around you. Do not complain of the tedious factory meetings where you will be harangued by Party functionaries and try not to doze off during the sessions of Marxist-Leninist instruction that will become a regular feature of your working life.

But, as we have said (see *Industrial Worker*), your chance may come, and you may be able to form genuine works councils in times of crisis and even have them negotiate genuinely with the Communist authorities—although they will eventually be suppressed unless the whole regime is overthrown.

Traitor, Quisling

There will, of course, be many high posts available throughout the police, governmental, and economic machinery for any reasonably qualified traitors. If you are lacking in any qualification, you can work your way upward, say through the ranks of the Seksoti or secret collaborators of the secret police, and you might emerge in the course of time with a satisfactory job in one of those unobtrusive organizations of American nationals under Soviet direction concerned with the pursuit, identification, and betrayal of your fellow citizens.

Travel Agent or Travel Agency Employee

Travel agencies as constituted at present will be shut down, but employment for a certain number of the redundant operatives may become available in local government, supervising the schedules of the crowded trains and buses. Here the principle will be that the lower the level of service, the more bureaucrats will be required.

Trotskyite

In your case the prognosis is so grave that your only alternative to flight would seem to be to prepare to die.

University Teacher (see *Academic*)

Veterinarian

Not only will the keeping of domestic pets be virtually discontinued, but the general scarcity of funds will mean that the treatment of those that remain will be undertaken at home. We suggest that you equip yourself to specialize in the care of horses and farm animals. There will always be a demand for the latter, and horses will proliferate as cars grow scarcer. You will become a government servant, and a comparatively well-paid one; that is, at about an eighth of your present salary. You must take care at all times that blame for the death of badly managed collective farm cattle is not pinned on you. Above all, if you can, avoid tending horses under Soviet ownership. Many vets were shot for alleged poisoning of Red Army horses in the 1930s, and even if it does not come to that, you could very easily be victimized.

Worker (see Trade Unionist)

Writer

Writers will know better than most people what to expect from the Occupation as they are already well informed as to what happens to their co-writers behind the Iron Curtain and in other Communist countries. If you wish to become a rich, celebrated conformist, you should, of course, begin to familiarize yourself without delay with socialist realism. Cultivate those Communists and Sovietophiles who are already prominent on the cultural scene and who will become your artistic commissars when the Russians arrive. Without their approval, your books are not going to be published, you will receive no literary prizes, and above all you will stand no chance of being included in any of the writers' delegations that visit other countries. This will not matter if the delegations are going to other Communist countries, as that would afford you little relief from the tedium of the life to which you are already condemned—a tedium that is particularly hard, we might add, for a writer. But occasionally such delegations will visit any countries that have not already been subjugated by the Soviet Union, and then you will have a brief chance, in spite of the secret policeman attached to your group, to see what life is like beyond the prison walls. Take a good look at it; there may not be many such glimpses left.

If you are a real writer, and you can somehow manage to emigrate to a free country before the Soviet army takes over, you should probably make up your mind to go. It will not be an easy decision. You will be reluctant to cut yourself off from your own roots, from your people in their hour of agony, from the sources of your inspiration. It is worthwhile consoling yourself with the thought that many writers before you have chosen to live as exiles and that in many cases emigration has not only not damaged but has actually sharpened their perceptions and intensified their art. We put forward one fact that may help you to decide. In *The Penguin Book of Russian Verse* (1962), we find that the average age at death of those writers who went into exile after the Russian revolution was seventy-two, whereas the average age at death of those writers who chose to stay behind was forty-five. The higher life expectancy of the exiles was twenty-seven years. (See also *Actor; Artist; Filmmaker; Musician.*)

Youth

You will find yourself under very heavy pressures of a type to which your present life has not accustomed you.

On the one hand, the Communist victors will hope above all to be able to harness the strength and spirit of the American young to their scheme of things. On the other, young people everywhere, although perhaps especially in America, have a tradition of nonconformity, rebellion against authority, a desire to think for themselves.

We would expect many American young people—especially those young enough not yet to have spouses or children—to throw themselves into the tens of thousands of spontaneous flare-ups of resistance that will mark the early days. Many will be killed, many captured and sent to labor camps. But there will be many survivors; some will join the partisans, and some will fade back into the background, having learned a bitter lesson.

To these latter, during the phase of consolidation of Communist power, we offer the same counsels of prudence we gave their elders. It will be much harder for the young and ardent to maintain the same restraints. You will make the effort. You will grow up, become tempered, and mature very quickly.

The special Communist effort to indoctrinate you will mean that you will be under considerably higher pressures than your elders. Membership of the Communist party itself will probably never be allowed to rise above a few million, and there will be no question of forcing adults, except in certain specialist posts, to join it. The Young Communist League, however, will number tens of millions, and for most jobs available to the young, and studentships at universities, joining will be almost unavoidable. This will mean that you will lose several hours a week at compulsory sessions in Marxism-Leninism, the Communist version of current events, and so forth, in addition to endless harangues about loyalty and the florious future, which you will be expected to applaud.

You will find that the youth leaders who serve the regime, and in particular the secretaries of the Young Communist League branches, are a more repulsive lot than even their adult equivalent. The sulky fanatic, the starry-eyed dupe, the weasel-faced careerist—and after a year or two there will be little to distinguish them—will feel their moral isolation, will lash out mercilessly at any sign of indiscipline, will be in the closest possible contact with the secret police (of which many of them, in fact, will be clandestine members). You will have to learn suspicion, caution, extreme self-control. As soon as the regime is consolidated you will be liable for conscription into the American People's Army, for a two-year term in peacetime, if any. Discipline will be incomparably tougher, pay lower, leave much rarer than in present day Western armies. Unless your class, family, and general background appear impeccable, you will be restricted to the infantry and need not expect a promotion. In wartime, young and active men who would otherwise have been sentenced to a labor camp will be inducted into "penal battalions" that will be used in particularly dangerous situations such as charging over enemy minefields. The survival rate will be low, but some who have served say that it was even preferable to the slow and mindless dying off in the labor camps.

But with all the casualties your generation will suffer, millions upon millions of you will survive. And on record, the Communists have never succeeded—in spite of appearances to the contrary—in carrying out their program of fully indoctrinating the young. You should remember that the vast majority of your age group, not only in America but throughout the Soviet world, is at heart disaffected. However much, over the years, your immediate needs take precedence, this core of your personality will remain. And you have one great point in your favor: unlike your parents, you may find that the overthrow of Soviet power will come when you are still in the full vigor of, perhaps, your forties, when you will provide the leaders to build a new America and a new world.

6

THE QUALITY OF LIFE

YOU WILL FIND the altered climate of your life hard to adjust to.

The first physical and psychological effects of the defeat, however it comes about, will be very terrible and will last months, perhaps years. You will have been shocked into a state of numbness that will rob many people of the will to live, against which you will have to struggle or succumb.

Then, as the Occupation tightens its grip, you will have to accustom yourself to the prospect of living a life that will be totally politicized. In all Communist countries, politics is an obsession, the central core of all thought and activity. You will find that your life is heavily bound up with questions of your own orthodoxy; with matters of heresy, schism, blasphemy, and back-sliding, and of the orthodoxy of the people around you. Not only will you be required to attend lectures on Marxism-Leninism at your place of work, but the newspapers you read, the television you watch, the radio you listen to, even the very streets around you will be filled with Communist slogans and exhortations. You will not be able to attend a football game or walk through a park without being subjected to propaganda speeches from massed loudspeakers. One particular irritation will be the visits of delegations from any still democratic countries, consisting of Communist sympathizers whose fulsome praise for the new order and the happiness of the Americans living under it will be sure to turn your stomach. Such things you will find maddening, but you must accustom yourself to them and put up with them, for to appear bored or hostile will be dangerous. After a time you will find that you hardly notice.

Outside your own home, perhaps even outside your own room in your own home, you feel yourself continuously subject to examination and scrutiny. It will be like living in a fishbowl. Or, to change the metaphor, you will feel as if you had been stripped of your clothes and are walking naked or as if the regime has performed a delicate operation on you that has peeled off the outer layer of your skin. As the Russian writer Isaac Babel remarked, under Soviet communism at its worst, "One only talks freely with one's wife—at night, with the blankets pulled over one's head."

You will find yourself forced to separate your life outdoors from your life indoors, your public life from your private one. You will begin to practice the compartmentalized existence practiced by all people who survive under a Communist dictatorship. You will split your mind into two halves. It is a trick that it will take you some time to acquire; but unless you belong to the minority, tiny and nasty, who will throw in their lot with the Communists, you will eventually learn how to demarcate your activities into a public sphere and an increasingly constricted private sphere. And you must get used to the fact that you will have to do or say something you will hate yourself for at least two or three times a day.

You will do all the things required of you: attend the meetings, march in the parades, chant the slogans, cheer the leaders.

You will at the same time perform an inner withdrawal and cultivate a very intense private life. This is where you must live—inside yourself or within a small circle—and it is a life that will become increasingly precious to you.

You will become gratified at the depth and closeness of your family relationships and your immediate friendships. These profound affections are the compensation, well known in all Communist countries, for the otherwise monotonous and mechanical quality of your existence. You will also find that, beneath the brusqueness and suspicion with which you will treat strangers and outsiders; beneath the endemic bad temper, snarling, and rudeness, there will sometimes spring up a remarkable spirit of kindness and generosity. Deprivation, fear, short rations, endless waiting lines, and the need to be servile will make everyone touchy and quarrelsome. Suspicion will arise between honest men. And yet, people who are companions in misery in their submission to a Communist government, even in Russia itself, are often prompted to behave toward each other with a rare selflessness and compassion.

However, take care not to be too carried away by the warmth of your friendships and family feeling. You will not really be safe even in the bosom of your own family. A specific and very great danger will arise when, after the regime is fully established, your children will have to join the "Pioneers" and will thus become integrated into the Communist system. In addition to providing some military training and running the summer camps, the Pioneers will inculcate the lesson that loyalty to Communism is far more praiseworthy than loyalty to one's family. As we have said, if you have subversive ideas, you must be very careful not to express them directly in front of your younger children. Even the most loyal child may inadvertently blurt things out and get you into trouble. Some children become brainwashed by the constant propaganda to which they are exposed and become zealous agents of the regime. Such unfortunate girls and boys are singled out and cherished by the Communists. Pavlik Morozov, a boy who during the collectivization of the land in the Soviet Union denounced his parents for hoarding and had them shot, is still lauded as a hero in the USSR and new statues to him have recently been erected. Most parents will try to pass on to their children, as we remarked earlier, decent values, and the general experience from Communist countries is that many succeed. However, you must proceed with the utmost vigilance, especially when your children are at an impressionable and talkative age. Therefore, as you peer out across the ruins, your first duty to yourself and to your loved ones is to practice caution. Every day you will be walking through a minefield. Every caretaker, doorman, porter, elevator man, lavatory attendant, and taxi driver is a potential government informer, not to mention the people with whom you regularly rub shoulders at the office or factory. You will have to consider very carefully the weaknesses of your old friends and acquaintances. And you must never make new friends impulsively or trust first impressions. Enlarge your circle slowly and carefully. You will learn to identify the people who are sympathetic to you and your ideas by subtle signs: a slight smile here, a cautious nod there. Even then you will be very careful. It is true that there may only be one rotten apple in the barrel; but you will not know which it is.

By the way, on the subject of communication, the telephone system will deteriorate rapidly, and you will no longer be able to rely on it to get through on any given day. However, we would advise you to keep your telephone if you can. A friend may be able to give you useful information that is otherwise unobtainable, for example, the appearance of lemons at some market. But do not speak indiscreetly. The chances of being bugged will be very small, especially at first; but as with all your actions, better safe than sorry should be your guiding principle. Similarly, you will not put on paper, in letters in particular, any facts or thoughts that might give offense to the authorities or annoy any individual official.

You might also think of having a radio capable of receiving stations overseas, which may give you better information about what is going on in the United States than you will be able to obtain from official broadcasts. In listening to these, you should also take the customary precautions of keeping the volume low and not having anyone present of whose reliability you are not certain.

There will be times of comparative relaxation as well as ones of intense horror. In these milder times, you still should not talk too freely. Remember that there is a file on you at the local secret police headquarters, and when things get worse again, you may suffer. As a Soviet writer rightly remarked to the American academic Dr. Gene Sosin when congratulated that things were a little easier. "Yes, but what about yesterday—and tomorrow?"

You may have complained, in your time, of the spread of bureaucracy in present-day America. When you come to look back upon it, you will be astonished at its moderation in comparison with what you will now experience. The number of forms to be filled in will increase tenfold. The number of permits, identity cards, labor books, ration cards, and registrations will astonish you. State offices will multiply, and the number of their employees will proliferate. But more importantly, from your point of view, is the fact that you will be entirely at the mercy of the new functionaries. There will be no press, independent lawyer, or politician, nor any other effective means of combating errors, injustices, and bullying. Courtesy toward the citizen will disappear. You will feel that you are mere bureau fodder. But be prepared for it. Get used to it. Study the new forms carefully. Do not be too alarmed if some document goes astray— very few people will be able to keep up fully with all the demands. On the other hand, if you are cheerful and helpful to your local administrators, who after all are subject to harassment in their turn, you may find them helpful when you want, for example, to visit a coastal state at short notice and thereby be able to get your permits in a week or ten days instead of having to wait months.

Inside every office the tension will be high. Those seeking promotion, or mere survival in their jobs, will increasingly tend to use every form of intimidation and blackmail against anyone they believe is a threat to them, including denunciation on charges of anti-Soviet agitation, which will lead to swift arrest. We can only advise you to keep a low profile and to control your natural instinct to express your own feelings and opinions. You will be able to console yourself by the frequent disappearance into labor camps of those who gained promotions only to find themselves denounced by even more devoted toadies of the regime.

Though the government apparatus will undergo a great expansion, all the key posts will be taken over by trusted supporters of the Soviets. However, there will be a transition period when the number of people with suitable training will be inadequate, and for a time, numbers of old civil servants will keep their jobs, although many will be purged, and those judged least politically reliable will be demoted or passed over for promotion. In the economic departments all who hold non-Marxist economic ideas will be removed. Salaries at the senior level will be high, with many perquisites such as cars, apartments, and so on; but the lower grades will suffer a sharp decline in real income. Moreover, although many buildings that have been abandoned by or seized from business firms will have been taken over, the expansion will be too great to cope with except by an increase in the numbers of people sharing an office. This should rise to between three and four times as many as now. Privacy is always one of the rarest commodities in a Communist dispensation. There will be a corresponding deterioration in office equipment. Nevertheless, government employ will be the only alternative for many persons who previously owned their own store or business concern or who were employed in one of the now-extinct enterprises.

There is something to be said, in fact, for seeking a job in one of the main offices dealing with the controls, permissions, and documentation now demanded on an ever-increasing scale. In such surroundings, it is easier to remain anonymous and to draw the minimum of attention to oneself—always an important consideration. On the other hand, a post in a small town, where there might be more opportunities for establishing relationships with those involved in the supplies of food and other necessities, has its points; moreover, it will always be advantageous to live where you do not need transport other than a bicycle to get to work. In the cities, where your home may be far from your job, the absence of private cars and the enormous overcrowding and erratic nature of public transport will make your morning and evening commuting a daily nightmare.

One problem that will particularly trouble you, especially during the initial period of disorganization, will be crime. Looters and muggers will have a field day. Because of the presence of the militia and the army patrols, you will not dare to carry anything that during a search might be construed as a weapon; but you and your family ought to make yourselves acquainted with at least the basic rules of unarmed combat in order to be able to defend yourselves against an attack by someone wielding a club, knife, or blackjack. In a fairly short time, however, the situation will ease. Muggers will disappear from the principal thoroughfares, and looters will be shot on the spot. The police will have full authority to fire on suspects however young, and there will be no public or other enquiries afterward.

However, once the immediate postoccupation crime wave has been put down, the authorities will cease to take much notice of nonpolitical crime. Occasional big round-ups of all known

153

criminals will put down particularly overt waves of crime, and those caught will be shipped off to labor camps to serve, as we have seen, as sub-bosses over the much more numerous "politicals."

But the police will be very busy, not only in all the many aspects of watching the citizens' loyalties, but also in a wide variety of administrative tasks such as issuing "internal passports," stamping them, registering all visitors to the particular town, issuing licenses for every sort of activity, and so on.

Soon a new criminal element will spring up. Many will be teenagers. Within a year or two America will have a well-developed caste of "hooligans." Some will be the veteran survivors of present teenage gangs who have neither been shot nor been incorporated into the "militia" of the new order. Many will be children and young adolescents, thrown into the streets upon the death or arrest of their parents, who will roam the towns and the countryside and commit savage crimes. As for the young thugs who have been taken on by the regime, you may even recognize them, if only from old newspaper photographs, as you see them in uniform, accosting and arresting you, and asking bribes for your release. Experience shows, moreover, that many such criminals become well adjusted to their work and are soon indistinguishable from their more ideological comrades. Several common criminals rose high in Soviet and Eastern European police organizations; one, E. G. Evdokimov, even becoming a member of the Party's Central Committee.

Organized crime in the form of the Mafia will be put down firmly; although any important member of the Mafia who shows any political sophistication ought to find it possible to arrange to be recruited into the regime's administrative machine. Official histories of Communist movements relate that even "bandit" groups were incorporated into the Party machinery, with the original leaders usually, but not always, being purged later. Such an arrangement would be of great help to an occupation

154

force without much of a base in the country, although the Mafiosi concerned would have to undertake to abandon crime except for actions on behalf of the Communist authorities.

Major crime rings that are nowadays unbreakable because of American legal provisions will not survive. But small-time crooks will seize the opportunities for bribery and fixing and acting as shady go-betweens offered by endless regulations and ill-paid bureaucrats. Soon, some will hardly be regarded as crooks at all by a population in desperate need of coping with the endless demands of officialdom. In fact, they will be treated almost as public benefactors. From time to time their actions will result in mass trials of fixers, crooks, and officials, leading in some cases to executions in the hope of a deterrent effect although without much long-term success.

So much for life as you will see it in your hometown. There will be many, in the uranium mines and elsewhere, who would return to it with joy. But what of the general prospects? At least, you may feel: "Better Red than dead." Things will not turn out to be so simple, and you and your fellow citizens will not henceforth escape, as you had hoped, the horrors of war. As we have noted, the draft will be reinstituted, and young men will be called upon to serve a stint of two to three years in the "peace-time" American People's Army. However, it is not likely that peace will prevail, and older men, if necessary to the age of forty and beyond, will also become liable for call-up, particularly in the event that China has not yet been attacked or that China has been attacked but is still carrying on a major guerrilla resistance. In that case, Moscow will be in great need of manpower. And, logically enough, Soviet aims will be best served by leaving Soviet troops to hold America and sending American young men, and the young of other Soviet satellites, to the war zone— under strict Soviet control, just as, at present, Cubans and East Germans are being used in Africa. In addition, if Chinese nuclear development has proceeded as projected, we may expect fusion bomb strikes on prime Soviet targets in America. In that case, America will not have avoided nuclear war by its surrender. But, in any case, such wars will become commonplace in the inevitable splits and schisms that will beset a communized, or largely communized, world.

If Chinese and other resistance is protracted, the Soviet army will be stretched so thin that the American People's Army may also find itself committed against local patriots in the jungles of Africa and South America. All the same, it is even more likely that they will be sent to reinforce the pro-Soviet Vietnamese Communists as they fight the Chinese on the Mekong. Thus the war objectors of the late sixties may after all find themselves in Southeast Asia as the elderly conscripts of the early nineties.

Even a world effectively conquered by the USSR would be, as we said, beset by an endless cycle of schisms and rebellions, fought with the utmost ruthlessness and with every available modern weapon. As early as 1944, Milovan Djilas, who was then a leading Yugoslav Communist, was told by a Soviet general that "when Communism has triumphed throughout the entire world, then warfare will take on an ultimate bitterness." We know that Stalin and the Communist chieftains of Eastern Europe planned an assault on Communist Yugoslavia itself, abandoned only because of their then overriding fear of the West. In Hungary in 1956, the first open clash came between two Communist-headed governments (together with a barely averted war between the USSR and Poland). In 1968, Communist Russia invaded Communist Czechoslovakia; and in the following year, full-scale battles between Communist Russia and Communist China were in progress on the Ussuri River, with all-out nuclear war a near thing. In 1978, the war between Communist Vietnam and Communist Cambodia occurred; and later the fighting between Vietnam and China. As the Soviet general told Djilas, eventually the proliferating sects and factions of communism "will undertake the reckless destruction of the human race in the name of the human race's greater 'happiness.'" You can be Red *and* dead!

The Soviet authorities, as they do in Russia today, will institute the most comprehensive and compulsory civil-defense programs. All civilians will be made to take part in regular drills and exercises. You will find these tedious and exhausting after your day's work; but pay attention to them, and take them seriously. These are not theoretical undertakings.

Whether you are a soldier or a civilian, in the army or out of it, you will not be allowed, any more than the inhabitants of the Soviet Union are, to move about freely. Restrictions on travel are a fundamental component of Communist life. As in Russia, it will not be easy to obtain leave to move from one city to another or to relocate. You will be issued an identity card or "internal passport" that you will be required to carry at all times. It will contain your photograph and extensive personal data and will consist of several pages to provide room to stamp in the details of all your movements. (As we have seen, the whole working population will also be handed individual "labor books," again with multiple pages, as your working record, including notes of any fines, warnings, admonishments, or disciplinary action taken against you. It will record each change of job, and when each book is filled up, it will be forwarded to the official archives before the issuing of a new one.)

If you are given permission to visit a strange town, particulars will be entered in your internal passport, and they will be noted by hotel receptionists or apartment-block caretakers for transmission to the local police station. Most readers will know already that in Communist countries all the rooms in the larger hotels are bugged and that major visitors are directed to such hotels. If you are a reasonably obscure personage, you should therefore avoid the big hotels and not only for economic reasons. In the smaller and cheaper ones, even the secret police do not have the resources for such action.

In Communist countries, and in America after the defeat, you will not expect your hotel, particularly one of the less expensive ones, to come up to the prewar American standard, and there are some items that you ought to get used to carrying with you if you are able to travel. These will include a tablet of soap, a clean towel, and a supply of toilet paper or the cut-up pieces of newspaper that for some time will do universal duty as toilet paper. Even the better hotels in Communist countries have had the plugs for the baths and basins stolen, so you might also take with you a couple of plugs of assorted sizes. An extra blanket and a tin of flea powder might also come in handy. In the hotels, as in most public buildings, you will not expect to find the elevators working, so be prepared to climb the stairs.

Your sense of isolation and depression in a strange town will be even greater than it is in your own, where at least you have your friends and your family and know your way around. In a strange town you will find the restaurants and places of amusement even drearier than at home.

If you do decide to leave your dismal room and go in search of whatever entertainment there might be, you could conceivably visit one of the local cinemas. The fare will be familiar. In the main feature, battalions of jolly Communists with shining faces, led by wise and stalwart Party members, may be shown ardently fulfilling the latest Five-Year Plan. You won't find it enthralling, and you will feel uncomfortable sitting in the cinema practically alone, except for some young couples busy necking and some old people soundly snoozing. In any event, in the early days, the curfew will begin at eight or nine o'clock, so once you have swallowed your watery stew and acorn coffee in the State cafeteria, it will hardly be worth your while to wander further abroad.

In your gloomy room, you can switch on the television if any, or the radio. Most of the programs will consist of primitive propaganda of the type you avoided by not going to the cinema.

Or you may be able to watch a game of football between two factory teams or between teams of the American People's Army, the Secret Police, and other state bodies, in which at least the usual doses of propaganda will only be injected during the breaks in the action, when you can turn the sound down while waiting for play to recommence.

Perhaps during halftime you may glance through the newspaper, *The New York Red Times* or the *Washington Truth*. You won't bother with the political pages, devoted to turgid and predictable analysis, falsified statistics, and verbatim reports of the latest bloated speeches by Party leaders; but you will probably turn directly to the end of the paper, to the small section containing the daily chess problem or the crossword puzzle (if such a frivolity is allowed), and you might check the stub of your ticket in the State lottery against the list of winners. The State takes the bulk of the money, and the winners receive only fairly small awards, but even that would be a welcome addition to one's budget and scanning the list does at least give you something to look forward to.

You might, of course, simply choose to go straight to bed and huddle up under that extra blanket you brought with you. You will not have dared to bring with you any of the pre-Occupation books, or "underground" typescript literature you may have at home. Nor, unless you are a fervid supporter of the Party, will you have weighed down your baggage with one of the ponderous, ill-printed social realist novels that are published by the millions but that only devotees of boredom ever bother to open. However, you can probably solace yourself (unless the management is saving power by an early turning off of the lights at the main switch), with a volume by some classical author that, though it may have been somewhat expurgated, is deemed to have redeeming social value.

Pleasant dreams.

7

RESISTANCE

I T IS POSSIBLE, if not very probable, that you are visiting
your strange city in connection with one or another of the
resistance activities that have sprung up and that are always
flaring up more or less sporadically thereafter.

There is no point in being starry-eyed about the scope and
possibilities of the American Resistance. What happened in
World War II and in the forty years afterward, both with regard
to resistance and counterresistance techniques, is not a reliable
guide. If resistance methods have grown more sophisticated, so
have the means of combating them. It will be a long struggle.
Resistance groups will rise and will be wiped out. It would be
foolish to expect that the attainment of American liberation is
likely to take less than a generation or two. The resistance group
with which you perhaps cast your lot will in all probability be
merely one of a myriad of bright bubbles that the Russians will
burst.

You, in your lonely room, are likely to be doing some small
but invaluable service like carrying a message between illegal

urban groups. But, in the early years, there will still be patriot partisans, like the Swamp Fox, Francis Marion, in mountains and forests, and you might be a courier, or scout, for these. One of us has some experience with partisans, and we venture some advice in this field.

The Partisan

Partisans can consist of as few as five people or as many as five hundred; obviously, the larger they become, the more they lose their irregular characteristics and take on the appearance of routine military formations.

In the early years of Soviet rule, there will be a great many bands of partisans, major and minor, prowling the vast back-country of the United States and Canada. At first sight, North America is ideally suited to partisan activity. Partisans will take to the forests of Colorado, Oregon, and Washington; to the mountains of Wyoming, Montana, and Idaho; to the canyons of Arizona and New Mexico; to the marshes and bayous of Louisiana and Florida.

There are an estimated nine million handguns and rifles in the possession of individual Americans. Many of their owners belong to gun clubs and know how to use them. The people who vanish into the wilderness soon after the surrender will have taken care to raid their local clubs' caches and the armories of the National Guard in order to carry off a mass of weapons and ammunition. Wherever possible, they will have raided their nearby military barracks and navy and air force installations, where these have survived or are uncontaminated by atomic attack, and will have acquired trucks, jeeps, half-tracks, and as much sophisticated combat material such as antitank missiles, mines, and grenades as they can load up and cart away.

The worst problem faced by the modern partisan, as in Afghanistan, is the armored helicopter gunship. These can be brought down without sophisticated SAMs; but small arms are not very effective, and heavier, though simple, rifle-type weapons work well. These will not be readily available, and military commanders should divert supplies while this is still possible.

The American partisans will be tough and vigorous people who will know the territory where they operate like the back of their hand. They will know how to make themselves scarce in it and the best places to hide the stuff that they steal. They will know every road and path and track. They will be ranchers or farmers or people from small- or medium-sized towns who are experienced hunters and fishermen. They will be able to ride a horse and repair any sort of machine. A few will have owned their own aircraft. Above all, many will come directly from the armed forces.

They will be resourceful and physically fit. Some of them, who have seen the war coming and will be aware of the need for knowledgeable leadership, will have specially hardened themselves by means of additional climbing, hiking, camping, trekking, and orienteering. They will have mapped out the best ski trails, particularly those that can be traversed at night. The more provident will even have made special trips to the larger libraries to seek out and make photocopies of the more important books and articles on irregular warfare such as Mao Tse-tung's *Primer of Guerrilla War* or General Alberto Bayo Giroud's *150 Questions for a Guerrilla.* As we have said, part of this material will be out-of-date, but it will still contain a tip or two that might save your life in an ugly situation.

It will be a temptation to band together into sizable groups. This will be a natural instinct, especially after the shock of an overwhelming defeat.

Yet a band of even fifteen or twenty partisans already begins to pose serious administrative problems. Larger units are only desirable when the circumstances are such that the enemy troops are tied down elsewhere and cannot concentrate against you. But, even when it is feasible to have larger units, do not attack regular Soviet troops unless you have an overwhelming advantage. Even more important than an advantage of numbers or position, never forget the advantage of speed. Have your operation finished before the Russians can call up an air strike or ground reinforcements. By such tactics, Afghans armed with rifles and grenades have destroyed tank detachments. The threat of such action has meant that even when superior Russian force makes a valley untenable, the Russians have nevertheless withdrawn after laying it waste for fear of attacks on their supply columns.

Indeed, the Afghans have shown that determined guerrillas in suitable country can effectively fight the enemy to a standstill. All the same, do not forget that the Afghans have certain advantages. They still have an open frontier to the south and are able both to evacuate their noncombatants and to receive a certain amount of supplies from abroad. These advantages are unlikely to be available to an American partisan force. Then again, the Afghans are trained from childhood for guerrilla fighting. They are ready for it both in the sense that they know their mountains from a scout or sniper's point of view, and they are expert in the weapons of the lone fighter; but also, they are psychologically ready for such a war when it comes. The answer for Americans must be that they are quick learners. At first, they will make mistakes and suffer disasters. After a while, the survivors will have had the experience for which nothing else is a substitute.

You will pick your targets with the greatest care. As far as possible, limit yourself to those related directly to the Russians. You will not help your fellow citizens if you make their already uncomfortable lives even more uncomfortable by destroying the power stations, dams, and other facilities on which they rely. If, for military or political reasons, it nevertheless seems necessary to carry out such actions, let the population know your reasons.

Never forget that they are liable to the most savage reprisals. Hostages will be taken and shot. You will have to judge the merits of an operation against the horrors that are bound to result. It will astonish you, at first, how remorselessly the Russians will behave—not only toward yourself, but toward your families, toward anyone brave enough to help you, and also toward the populace at large. They have always done so, and now there will be little or no world opinion to influence what is going on. The Russians can act as they like: that is to say, as they acted in Lithuania and the Western Ukraine and as they are now acting in Afghanistan, or worse. Their ultimate argument was, and remains, the tank and the firing squad.

Nevertheless, even in cases where the prospects are poor, where the Russians can hunt you down in your forests, starve you out in your swamps, and bottle you up in your canyons, you will remember that elsewhere groups are holding out, fighting back; that you are part of a great national effort.

You will have advantages over your comrades in the cities. You will be able to operate your radios fairly freely; you might possibly be able to arrange for supplies to be smuggled in from abroad. Yet yours will not be an easy lot. The vast landscape in which you feel at home will sometimes seem to have turned into a prison. You will become more and more hardened physically and psychologically; yet your strength will also be sapped by the climate, whether hot or cold, wet or dry. You will have difficulties with food supplies. The winters will be hard.

All the same, hold out. Do not at any time be tempted to parley with the Russians under a flag of truce. In 1945, the Polish underground leaders contacted the Russians. They were guaranteed safe-conduct but were immediately arrested and later tried and sentenced for anti-Soviet activity. In 1956, the Hungarian minister of war was induced to attend talks with the Red Army commander in Hungary. He too was arrested, tried, and hanged. American partisan chiefs are likely to get an even shorter shrift, so do not weaken. It seems a more enviable fate to die fighting on Pike's Peak than in a cellar in Pittsburgh.

Partisans, generally speaking, cannot hold out forever unless they are aided from outside. Nevertheless, it has often taken a number of years even for the Communists, totally uninhibited as to methods, to destroy guerrilla movements even in comparatively small areas. The Lithuanian partisan struggle, in a small, well-forested but nonmountainous territory, was not abandoned till eight years had gone by. The same applies to the western Ukrainian partisans, in the more mountainous regions of the north Carpathians. In the larger territories of America, a longer struggle could probably be sustained, even though we may set against this the advantages of new Russian equipment.

It may be improbable that the Soviet system could be shaken to the point of collapse in so short a period. But nothing is impossible, and in the case of mass risings throughout the Soviet empire, American partisans could play a big part. In the more likely event that partisan warfare becomes ineffective long before the Soviet grip is shaken, it may be better for the partisan command to make a conscious decision to demobilize their surviving fighters, providing them with false papers and cover stories and fitting them into properly chosen backgrounds—as in both Lithuania and the Ukraine.

By that time, survivors would be few. If you are among them, you will act out the life of a loyal Soviet-American citizen and await your time. It may not come in your lifetime, but you can go to your grave with a clear conscience.

Good luck!

In the cities, and other areas easier to control than the mountains and forests, armed resistance will be difficult. For a few months, "urban guerrillas" in very small groups may succeed in carrying out sporadic acts of assassination and sabotage against the occupiers. But such groups have never succeeded in maintaining themselves for long in Communist-occupied countries. It may be that, in the special circumstances of America, such groups will last longer. But in a comparatively short time, at any rate, the complete ruthlessness of Communist secret police methods, involving in each case the probable arrest and torture of hundreds of people who might conceivably know anything, will probably have its effect. The illegal possession of a weapon will, in itself, in the early stages, carry the death penalty and, even later, will always involve sentencing to a labor camp even in the absence of any suspicion of rebellious intent.

Nevertheless, there will be Americans who feel impelled to strike back in this way. And, in spite of the disadvantages, some good results may yet be attained. Our advice is: Do not waste your efforts. A single, really massive act of sabotage against a carefully picked secret police or military target may be worthwhile; wrecking the odd train will not. The assassination of local, and if possible, of more important Quislings is also worthwhile, both in cheering the population and frightening the rulers.

After a few years, though, armed resistance in the cities on any organized basis will be virtually extinct. The resentments of the American people will not.

In fact, in all the countries that have come under Soviet occupation, the population has never become reconciled to the regime. The rulers have maintained support only from that small caste that has done well in terms of power and privilege and from a limited gang of indoctrinated young thugs. The sheer pervasiveness and ruthlessness of the secret police and the whole power apparatus is enormous. But only armed force, including the Soviet army itself and the prospect not merely of defeat but of greatly intensified military terror, has kept the people down.

Even so, time after time, whole populations have come together in great movements of resistance and rebellion that have at least temporarily thrown off the Soviet yoke.

Among Americans, with their special attachment to the principles of liberty, their special horror of foreign rule, you may expect that Communist control will never even begin to strike serious roots. People will be cowed, baffled, disorganized. Some may even hope to work "within" the new system and turn it in a more acceptable direction. But the invariable experience has been that Communist policies increasingly antagonize every section of the population—including major sections of the Party itself, who see that they cannot rule indefinitely on such a basis.

Even in democracies, governments become unpopular. And they would become even more unpopular if they stayed in power, even without terror, for a decade or decades. How much more is this true of an unpopular foreign-sponsored clique, bound by its principles to ever more hated and unsuccessful policies. A poll taken in Czechoslovakia at the end of 1967 showed that the then leaders of the Party and State had the support of 1 percent of the population.

The situation that will thus be established, throughout the Soviet empire, is that of a population faced with a political and military machinery developed over many years for the purpose of holding down resentment and preventing its expression. And of crushing it if, in spite of everything, it turns into full rebellion.

Yet as the years go by, you will sooner or later find yourself swept up in a mass movement against the occupier. These movements are very often started in the cities, in the form of strikes and demonstrations by the industrial workers (see p. 95). With no trade union rights, yet thrown closely together by the nature of their work, they are the first to be able to make some united protest at a reduction in the rations (or mere absence of necessary foods in the market), at deteriorating housing conditions, or sudden cuts in piece-rates—all of which have always, sooner or later, appeared in cities under Communist regimes. This is not, of course, the only way in which pent-up resentments will be released; some gross offense to national pride has also been the last straw in bringing people out onto the streets. In any case, after years of repression, during which you may have felt that no one else thought as you did, it will be immensely refreshing to find the bulk of the population coming together as comrades in a struggle.

It will be particularly encouraging to note that the young, right down to school children, whom you feared might have been indoctrinated and lost to their country, are the most active and aggressive.

In the beginning, there will be little question of armed uprising. The few weapons secreted here and there will be no match for the machine guns and cannon of the police and soldiers. It will be a matter of furious but unarmed demonstrations, run by spontaneously formed and secret committees, that will march with various demands on Party headquarters and the local government buildings.

The authorities will find that units of the Sovietized "U.S. Army" will refuse to fire on their compatriots. Secret police and eventually Soviet army formations will, perhaps not until your town has been in your own hands for some days, put down the crowds with machine-gun fire. Losses in your town at this stage may not be very great—probably only a few hundred dead. If, as is probable, you survive as "order" is being restored, you will face something similar to the problems of the very first phase of the Occupation.

If the resentment thus boils up spontaneously in a single city, the regime will probably find it possible to isolate it. In this case, it will be comparatively easy to crush the movement. Nevertheless, it will prove worthwhile. The rulers' morale will have been shaken. The American people, even if not at once, will learn of your exploit. One more hand will have taken up, and will be passing on, the torch of liberty.

In other circumstances, the movement may spread from city to city before it can be stopped, till a mass rising of the American people faces the Communists in Washington.

All the advantages will still be on the side of a well-armed, well-organized military force. All the same, the mere numbers of the insurgents, their ability, with luck, to halt essential supplies to the occupier, the coming over to them of portions of the puppet "U.S. Army," will present the Russians with a formidable threat. Even so, the chances are heavily against you. If the United States, well equipped with modern arms, was unable to defeat the Soviets, it will be even more difficult now. Although they may have a period of indecision (when they hope that the movement can be headed off), when they act, it will be with complete ruthlessness, and all weapons deemed necessary will be employed.

Casualties will be heavy, and the immediate reprisals heavier still. But they will not be able to deal with everyone who has opposed them since that will involve almost the entire population. In similar circumstances, even quite prominent resisters have escaped the net.

And there will be advantages. First, the whole Communist network will have been shaken and virtually destroyed; the building of a new Party on the discredited ruins of the old will be no easy business. Second, the Russians will wish to ease the tensions and return things to something similar to Soviet-style "normality" as soon as they can. To this end, they will, after the first wave of terror, withdraw the most ruthless and hated of their American servants and replace them with men of more moderate appearance. Economic policies that have driven the population to desperate acts will be to some extent relaxed.

But above all, the American people will once more be morally invigorated. Over the years that follow, it will look as if, once again, apathy and adaptation have set in; but the example will not really be forgotten. Sooner or later, perhaps not in your own lifetime, the Soviets will be faced by a national rebellion at a time when their grip on the rest of their empire is being shaken, and their internal policies have brought the Soviet Union itself to catastrophe.

AFTERWORD

IF YOU HAVE followed us thus far, you are no doubt shocked and gloomy. What can we say to cheer you up?

Our advice on how to behave under Soviet rule will generally improve your chances of survival. But even if you survive, the prospects are grim enough, for the scenes we have described are not imaginary. They have happened elsewhere. They will happen in the United States if its leaders misunderstand Soviet motives, or if they make miscalculations in their foreign policy.

We live in dangerous times. Such miscalculations are very possible. But they are not inevitable.

The American people and their representatives have it in their power to prevent their country from undergoing the ordeal we have described. A democratic government, with all its distractions and disadvantages, is still the most effective method that men and women have yet devised for deciding policy. It is not infallible, it is slow to learn, and it is willing to grasp at comfortable illusions; but it may yet act decisively. If it does not, its ideals may yet prove ineradicable. We would guess that even in the depths of defeat, invasion, and occupation, the memory of what democracy has meant to Americans will not perish. Men and women will remember that their parents and grandparents once lived in hope and freedom and will determine to wrest the same for their own children and grandchildren. The recollection of that lost democracy will sharpen the longing for it. It is when Americans have been most cruelly and thoroughly collectivized that they will yearn most fiercely to regain their individuality. The more the Soviet absolutists and their allies suppress the individual, the more they will nourish him.

But why should we fear that such an ordeal may face us? The economic potential of the West in gross national product is far greater than that of the Soviet Union. In a direct comparison between the United States and the USSR, the Soviet GNP (in 1981)—and for a larger population—was about 1,500 billion dollars as against the American 3,000 billion dollars. The GNP of the NATO countries (and France) was about 5,700 billion dollars against the Warsaw Pact's 1,800 billion dollars. And that is to say nothing of the other allies and friends of the West: Australia, New Zealand, Japan, and Brazil alone add another 1,400 billion dollars, while the contribution of Russia's allies outside the Warsaw Pact is negligible. Even the population of the NATO countries is greater, with 554.8 million against the Warsaw Pact's 365.7 million. And, with all the deficiencies of the Western effort, military manpower is not much less than that of the Warsaw Pact: 4.8 million as against 5.2 million.

In fact, the Soviet Union is economically far behind the United States. American technology is always a generation ahead of theirs. They have to turn to the United States for wheat. The Soviet economy is at a dead end. The Communist system has failed to win support in any of the countries of Eastern Europe. The Soviet idea has no attractions. On any calculation—of economic power or social advance or intellectual progress—

there could be no question of the Russians imposing their will. But in terms of actual military power, the West's advantage does not seem to have been made use of. It is at least matched, and many would say overmatched, in the nuclear field; the Western forces in Europe have less than half the striking power of their opponents. It is no good our being more advanced than they are if this is not translated into power—both military power and political willpower. As a leading British student of Soviet matters, Professor Hugh Seton-Watson, has said, the fact that a man is a more advanced creature than a crocodile will not be of much use to him if he goes swimming naked in the Nile.

How can they be a threat—a threat to the mere existence of the United States?

Because they have made an armament effort wholly disproportionate to their economic capacity. Because they have developed techniques of expansion through puppets. Because they have maintained a single-minded, long-term intention to press forward. Because the West misunderstands this.

Yet democracy has been underrated before. Its ideals—the urge to be free, to live one's life in one's own way without the bullying interference of the State—are built into the human psyche, especially in America. It may yet wake to the problem.

Just as the airlines hope that their passengers will never have to follow the instructions they give you on what to do in case of a disaster, so we, for our part, hope you may never have to follow the advice we have given you in the preceding pages. But time is running short. We would be deceiving you if we pretended that the nightmare we have described is not a real and deadly possibility. If it does come about, we have one last piece of advice:

BURN THIS BOOK.